YOUR NEW JOURNEY

HOW TO THRIVE IN GRADUATE SCHOOL

AS A PERSON OF COLOR

AJ Cade

America's Historian
Maryland

America's Historian LLC
Maryland
www.americashistorian.com

Copyright © 2023 – Anthony J. Cade II

All rights reserved. No part of this book may be used or reproduced in any manner whatsoever without written permission except for brief quotations embodied in critical articles or reviews. Published by America's Historian LLC, Maryland, United States of America. First Edition. Hardcover.

Thank you for buying an authorized edition of this book and for complying with copyright laws by not reproducing, scanning, or distributing any part of it in any form without permission. You are supporting writers and their hard work by doing this.

Cover Design by Anthony J. Cade II
Published in the United States of America.
First Printing Edition, 2023

Library of Congress Cataloging-in-Publication Data
Cade II, Anthony J. 1988-
  Your New Journey: How to Thrive in Graduate School as a Person of Color

LCCN: 2023944324

ISBN: 979-8-9888417-2-2

TABLE OF CONTENTS

List of Illustrations & Tables vii
    Illustrations vii
    Tables vii

Disclaimer viii
Dedication ix
Introduction x
    Who am I? x
    Who is this Book For? xii
    What Will You Learn? xiii

Chapter 1: A Lonesome Journey 1
    Your Superpower 3
    Diversity in Academia 5
    Women in Academia 9
    Academic Circles 11
    Diverse Universities 14
    Mental Preparation is Half the Battle 15
    NFG 18

Chapter 2: Establishing a Support System 21
    Group Support to See You Through 24
    Leaning on Loved Ones 27

Table of Contents

    Campus Support Team 31

    Give as Much as You Get 34

    Funding Your Academic Career 35

Chapter 3: Developing Your Goals 41

    Developing Your Personal Goals 46

    Developing Your Professional Goals 47

    Developing Your Academic Goals 52

    Maintaining Your Motivation 53

Chapter 4: Choosing the Right University 57

    Start with Your University & Your Major 58

    The Devil is in the Details 63

    Time to Apply 69

    Academic Advisors: An Underutilized Resource 75

    Decision Time! 77

Chapter 5: Starting Graduate School 80

    Operating Expenses 81

    A Plan for Every Year 83

    Roll Call! 85

    An Imposter is Among Us 88

    The Backbone of Graduate Study 93

    Let Off Some Steam 94

Chapter 6: Getting Your Master's 99

Paths to Graduation 101

Which One? 104

Forming a Graduate Committee 105

Writing Your Thesis 110

Is Publication Important? 112

Graduate Certificates 117

Peer Support 119

Chapter 7: Earning Your Doctorate 122

Making the Right Choice 123

What is a PhD Committee? 125

Comprehensive Exams: What to Know 128

Nailing Your Comps 130

Crafting Your Prospectus 136

From Research to Dissertation 140

Support Systems: The Gift that Keeps on Giving 146

Chapter 8: Taking the Next Step 150

Now What? 151

Career Prospects 155

Resume Crafting 164

The Imposter Returns 181

Chapter 9: Being Your Own Boss 187

Building an Empire 189

Table of Contents

Legal Responsibilities 193

Taking It to the Next Level 197

Freelancing 199

Picking a Niche & Method 201

Becoming an Authority 203

Motivational Speaking 205

Scaling Up 208

In Closing 212

Seek out Financial Literacy 212

Avoiding Burnout 213

Is Freedom Free? 219

Believing in Yourself 222

LIST OF ILLUSTRATIONS & TABLES

Illustrations

1. Maslow's Hierarchy of Needs (p 22)
2. Non-Specific vs. Specific Goal (p 42)
3. Deciding on Your University & Major (p 59)

Tables

1. Differences Between an MA and PhD (p 53)
2. Organizing Information on Your Potential Universities (p 63)
3. Resume Example (p 169)
4. Skills & Work Experience Annotation (p 174)
5. Understanding Business Structures (p 194)

DISCLAIMER

The views and opinions expressed inside this book are solely of the author, Anthony J. Cade II, and America's Historian LLC. They do not reflect the Federal Government, the Department of Defense, or any corporate entity mentioned, nor have they provided any endorsement of this text. All questions and concerns about the following hardcover should be forwarded to America's Historian LLC, Maryland.

Thank You

DEDICATION

I dedicate this work to my children, Cordell, Anthony, Peter, and Zara. They inspirited me to complete my PhD, and I hope this work inspires children like them on their journey.

INTRODUCTION

So you are considering applying to graduate school in pursuit of a master's, doctorate, or an alternative graduate degree? **Good for you!** This is your new journey, one that should be paved towards a subject or field of you choose out of love, and it is a choice that could fulfill you for the rest of your life if properly thought out.

Going through the higher education enrolment process is quite stressful, but what happens when you feel underrepresented, unheard, or like an imposter? Graduate school can feel like a cumbersome journey for many people who come from traditionally underrepresented groups in academia. Between wanting to do right for others, feelings as if you are by yourself, and feeling like you just do not fit in at graduate school, the pressure can be crippling. However, it does not have to be that way. If you are holding a copy of this book, you have already taken the first step towards ensuring your journey into and through graduate school is one where you will thrive.

Who am I?

My name is Dr. Anthony J. Cade II, but all my friends call me AJ. Because you purchased one of my first books, you can consider yourself one of my friends, and I invite you to address me as AJ as well. I am a medically retired United States Marine with multiple combat deployments to my name. I earned an associate's, bachelor's with honors, and two master's degrees before my obtaining my PhD. I love history, working out, technology, writing, and animals. Most importantly, I am a father to four beautiful children, and similar to my kids, I hope to guide you along your journey to success.

When I write about feeling underrepresented in graduate school, I mean it literally. I was the only veteran in my cohort for all my graduate degrees. I was the only person willing to disclose I had a medical disability, one severe enough that it forced me to retire from the Marines. I was the only married man with children as well. I was even the only one working full-time in my chosen field during my doctoral studies. I was also the eldest person in my cohorts. However, what shocked me more than any of that was that I was also the only Person of Color in my incoming graduate cohorts. I do not write these words to reproach any university of impropriety, but I do write all of that to make it clear: I know what it means to look around the room and think to myself, "I am the only one."

After touring hundreds of universities across the world for various speaking engagements—and meeting undergraduates and graduates who felt as I did—I crafted the following guidebook for individuals from all walks of life who plan to or are already in graduate school and feel as if they are an outlier with little to no assistance toward their success. As your friend, I want you to know that I am here for you, and I want to give you all the tools you may need to complete your journey.

Who is this Book For?

This book is for anyone who has ever felt marginalized or as if their voice did not matter. For first-generation students who do not have family members or friends to pass on knowledge and experience. *Your New Journey* is for people from diverse and culturally rich backgrounds who doubt themselves in a predominantly white, male-dominated education system. This is for those unaware of the level of diverse excellence in abundance inside of higher education. Most importantly, it is for those of you who feel like an outsider in academia.

If you want to move through the phases of graduate school without feeling weighed down by a demographic on a piece of paper, then this is for you. If you would like to know how to cultivate your voice, find a support system, and develop a feeling of inclusivity amongst your peers, this book is definitely for you.

Finally, if you are ready to broaden your horizons and achieve the success you have always envisioned for yourself—the success you are undeniably worthy of—this book is for you.

What Will You Learn?

Your New Journey is about cementing your position as a graduate student and a professional in this modern era. This book examines uncomfortable topics and shines a light on some of the systematic racism prevalent in higher education. However, you will arm yourself with tools that will help you cultivate your circle of trust to combat this system, and this book will ultimately help you to complete graduate school with a map for your future afterward.

You are the master of the future. You command your destiny. You have the power to be anything you desire, and it is all in the palm of your hands. It might be a cliché, but to say the world is your oyster is an understatement. It is imperative that you know this as we move on, and you keep that thought in your head throughout your academic journey. As you read this hardback, I want you to continually remind yourself that you will thrive during and after graduate school, and if so, by the time you finish reading, you will have the mindset and the tools necessary to do so.

Above all else, working your way through graduate school takes grit, mental resilience, and dedication. Several techniques inside this book can help you hone all of these abilities.

Introduction

Here is a quick run-through of what I will be covering:

- How your unique background is your secret superpower.
- How establishing a support system early on will help you through your difficult days.
- Why developing your goals—on both a professional and personal level—will keep you motivated.
- Force you to ask yourself, do I need graduate school?
- How choosing the right university can impact your experience and career prospects.
- How to navigate the early days of graduate school.
- How to pursue your master's or doctorate degree.
- The art of crafting a resume.
- Why starting a business or a freelancing career might be the next best step for your career.

I purposely set up this book for you to read and return as needed. It is your one-stop shop for your entire graduate school journey! Everything you need to thrive in and after graduate school is included here, so do **not** lose this book.

We have a long and exhilarating road ahead of us, so let us begin.

A LONESOME JOURNEY

Graduate school—by design—is the place where you feel tested to your limits. Not only are the demands of academia more intense than undergraduate study, but you also have to contend with feeling alone in a place that originally was not designed for you to succeed. It can make you feel like nobody knows what you are going through. However, your unique situation presents you with an opportunity that most of your peers do not have. Namely, only you can complete this journey, and none of your peers will see the world as you do. Furthermore, there will be this insidious little voice in your head that tells you that you are not meant to be there; however, the truth is nearly everyone has that voice—even your professors. That voice will be there throughout your journey, so do not feel as if you are going crazy. Instead, realize that you have a lot of preconditioning from a young age which you must let go of. When you have spent your whole life getting the side eye for being in a certain place or felt unaccepted for who you are, it is hard to let go of that narrative in your mind. Simply put, you have been through enough to know which situations you will feel welcomed and which you are going to feel uncomfortable. It is a perfectly normal survival mechanism.

Chapter 1

However, you are not reading this book to simply survive.

You are here to thrive.

So, we first need to work on your self-confidence and self-love. You need to tell yourself, "I **am** meant to be here. I **am** worthy of being here." Focus solely on this and yourself at the beginning of your new journey. Anything else will put too much pressure on you without producing positive results. There may be expectations for you to do well as the sort of "ambassador" for everyone back home or others with similar backgrounds to your own. There is this idea that if one of us succeeds, we can blaze the trail for all of us to do the same. This is amazing, and it certainly does help kids and others to know if they have a similar goal that it is obtainable if they work hard. However, the expectation that you will personally resolve decades—possibly centuries—of systemic issues alone is too much for one person to bear at the onset of their career. This is just as much your journey as it is about uplifting your community. It is more your journey than anything else. It is not selfish to focus on your success before considering how you can assist others to thrive. Save altruism for the end and focus on yourself at the onset. You freely give kind and encouraging words to others, tell yourself those exact words daily and remind yourself that you can and will succeed when you feel alone.

Your Superpower

As human beings, storytelling has always been our way of connecting and passing on essential information. Before history and knowledge were recorded on a cave wall, it was spread orally. Stories connect us. They unite us and help us find common ground with one another. This has remained the same in our modern world. Today, we bond over movie characters we have fallen in love with, share a mutual loathing of villains, and discuss the character's archetypes in our beloved books. Stories make the world go around while connecting everyone in it.

With that in mind, consider how your story conveys you as someone who is unique and has an inimitable perspective. Your background is fascinating and unlike so many others who came before you. It represents strength and the power of determination. You have a fantastic opportunity to tell a story your peers will never experience. Thus, it is a story nobody else in your department can tell or research. If there are commonalities with your peers, that will be a window for you all to connect, but your unique viewpoint gives you an approach toward research that ensures you stand out from the rest.

Past the point of connection, your unique paradigm allows you to generate new ideas. That is the whole point of diversity. When you have a bunch of similar people with similar views, they will problem-solve in similar fashions.

Chapter 1

While their ideas will be unique to each individual, there will be a common thread that might not allow them to see beyond those shared perspectives. You have a different view of the world, which can make problem-solving on your own and in a collaborative setting more productive and rewarding. Lean in on that, and embrace the times when you have different answers from the rest. Revel in the instances where you do not agree with everyone else, and when it is all said and done, know you carved out your path for success.

It is essential to note that, historically, people from underrepresented backgrounds are seen even less in higher education; this is not lost on your administrators or supervisors. As you move through life, you will see that while there is always going to be one "bad egg" who hopes you fail in every situation you enter, most of your supervisors want you to thrive. They understand the importance of you being in graduate school, not just for you and your community, but for the betterment of the university in question. Whenever you start to feel as though you do not belong, reassure yourself of how much you are wanted and needed right where you are. If that is not enough, remember that AJ and his guidebook are always here for you, and most importantly, fuck those small-minded people. I doubt they are worth the effort to think about, so ignore them and thrive in spite of their hate.

Diversity in Academia

Now, let us talk about a few of the countless pioneers you can admire during your journey. These people proved they were academics, scientists, poets, writers, and inventors first, and their background was secondary to their success, even though the struggle to climb the ranks was not lost on them. They persevered in spite of fear, intimidation, condemnation, and belittlement. They all decided to be the best versions of themselves—regardless of the implied or literal cost.

Take Mae Carol Jemison as a prime example of the ability to overcome the challenges of her time, challenges which still silently pervade our society today. As a child, Jemison always dreamed of becoming an astronaut. She was an incredibly bright, creative, determined child. This paid off in a big way for her by the time the 70s rolled around. In 1973, Jemison became one of the only black female students at Stanford University. She was only 16 years old at the time by the way. Can you imagine what it felt like as a young girl of color surrounded by mainly older, white men? One would assume she felt intimidated—perhaps a little out of place. On the contrary, Jemison attributes her success in moving through that phase of her educational journey to being young and, in her words, "a little arrogant." After graduating as a medical doctor, it took another fourteen years and a move from her medical internship, to becoming a peace corps doctor, and finally settling in Los Angeles to open her practice for her to return to her childhood dream. In 1987, Mae Carol

Chapter 1

Jemison became the first female astronaut of color, selected from over 2,000 applicants.

Edward Alexander Bouchet, the most famous PhD holder you have possibly never heard of, was born in 1852. How fitting is it that Bouchet was born the same year that prolific social reformer and statesman Frederick Douglass delivered his "What to the Slave is the Fourth of July?" Not only did Bouchet become the first Man of Color to earn a PhD in the US, but he was also one of the first American men to earn a PhD in physics. Up until his graduation, only twenty other Americans held this distinction. Despite ranking sixth in his graduating class at Yale University, Bouchet had a hard time finding his footing in academia. Nevertheless, he went on to teach physics and chemistry at the Cheyney University of Pennsylvania, then known as the Institute for Colored Youth, for twenty-six years. His works were greatly renowned, and Yale University acknowledged his contribution to their institution and to science overall, when they created a tombstone and placed it on what was once his unmarked grave. It may have been eighty years too late, but this legendary man has been receiving his due credit ever since. His name now posthumously adorns illustrious institutions, awards, and honor societies around the world.

Born a few years after Bouchet was William Edward Burghardt Du Bois, better known to many of us as W. E. B. Du Bois. Du Bois began his undergraduate journey at Fisk University in Nashville before applying to Harvard University in 1888. His Fisk credits were not recognized, and Du Bois had to go through an undergraduate program again—something he rather enjoyed because he was enthralled by academics. Du Bois used all of his inheritance as well as loans from friends and money earned from summer jobs to pay his way through Harvard, graduating cum laude in 1890. In 1891, he began his graduate studies in sociology at Harvard. As a budding academic and professor, Du Bois challenged one of the most prominent Black figures, Booker T. Washington. Du Bois' desire to see an equal and fair society—along with his exposure to violent segregate laws and penalties during his time in the South—spurred him to fight for what he believed to be right. Du Bois had no care or concern for Washington's status amongst the greater Black community or amongst the elitist whites. His only concern was with justice and equality. He was a historian, a sociologist, an author, an editor of the aptly named NAACP magazine, *The Crisis,* and a champion for the people. His contributions to society on the whole, the sheer number of important movements that he was involved in, and the volume of his authored works, are shown in the seemingly never-ending roster of accolades and accomplishments that Du Bois has to his name.

Albert Einstein, perhaps one of the most famous scientists of all time, was a German-born immigrant who became an American late in life. Born in March 1879 in Germany, his family moved to Italy and Switzerland during his childhood. In 1896, he entered the Swiss Federal Polytechnic School in Zurich, and he soon renounced his German

Chapter 1

citizenship for Swiss. After completing his PhD and publishing numerous groundbreaking theoretical works that still impact modern-day physics—and earning a Nobel Prize—Einstein applied to regain his German citizenship, which he held for several years before renouncing it again. During the interim, he left Germany for the United States to escape antisemitism which was prevalent at that time. Einstein accepted a position at Princeton and later became an American citizen in 1940. He held dual citizenship with the United States and Switzerland until his death in 1955. Einstein never let the waves of racism and xenophobia he encountered slow his trajectory or block his path toward greatness. It was Germany who lost Einstein, not Einstein who lost Germany, and you should take a similar approach during your journey. If you encounter an institution or country working against you, know it is their loss, not yours.

Finally, we come to one of the most world-renowned names and faces of all time: Martin Luther King Jr. Born in 1929, the incredible man that we affectionately call MLK was a graduate of Morehouse College, Crozer Theological Seminary, and Boston University. His activism and organizational leadership from 1955 up until his assassination in 1968 are lengthy and decorated. As a winner of the Nobel Peace Prize for his dedication to nonviolent resistance and the holder of a PhD in systematic theology, MLK was dedicated to the pursuit of knowledge. He was unwavering in his commitment to his beloved wife, Coretta Scott King, and their daughter, Yolanda Denise King. He was relentless in his cause to better the lives of all People of Color and Black equality across all areas of life—including education. He always felt that education was a path for People of Color to advance themselves, and I hope you take his lessons to heart.

These are just a handful out of thousands of notable people who have changed the world for the better through their pursuit of knowledge and education. The mountain that stands before you might seem insurmountable from the base, but it will be well worth it at the summit.

Women in Academia

Women have been the most marginalized group of people in human history. Irrespective of race, women have always had a harder time navigating academia—particularly Women of Color. Despite the hindrances, countless women have forged ahead. The 1800s were abuzz with historic firsts, and Elizabeth Blackwell was right there getting her slice of the pie. As the first woman to earn her MD from New York's Geneva Medical College, Blackwell was no stranger to being ostracized from a profession due to her gender. After sorrowfully watching her closest friend die, she turned to medicine. However, this was not her first move into academia as she and her sisters had—up until that point—been running their very own language school to alleviate their parents from abject poverty.

Chapter 1

In the 1900s, women continued to soar, with Chien-Shiung Wu leaving her native China to further her studies at the University of California-Berkeley. She earned her PhD in physics in 1940, and she was one of the key team members on the Manhattan Project—the secret program that developed the atomic bomb during World War II. Wu conducted dozens of experiments during her time at Berkley, and she disproved the theory of symmetry in physics. Wu was a brilliant, driven woman whose passion for physics led to several breakthroughs in the field.

Katherine Johnson was another woman in STEM, one who left a noticeable void when she passed in 2020. As a young girl, Johnson showed a deep interest in mathematics. She loved numbers and, in her words, would "count everything." She was always counting, from the steps up to the church, which she attended with her parents, to the number of steps it took her to get from the driveway to the front door. At the tender age of 15, she enrolled at West Virginia State College. She was great with names as well as faces, taking the time to learn who practically everyone on campus was and what they did. Her professor, Dr. William W. Schiefflin Claytor, was the third African-American to earn a PhD in mathematics, and he saw a bright spark in young Johnson. Clayton helped Johnson develop the necessary skills to become a research mathematician. As young as she was, she knew how profound this mentorship was. Eager to make the most of the fact that she was handpicked as one of three Black students to attend West Virginia's graduate school, she seized the opportunity.

Although she did not finish her degree, she used her education and skills to join NASA, becoming responsible for the trajectory of the first human space flight. She was awarded an honorary doctorate for her years of work in 2016 from her alma mater.

Today, we have so many women to look up to in academia, and each demonstrates that although there are obstacles, they are not insurmountable.

There are so many women like them—unique in their pursuits, but all paving the way for women in academia. You could be next. **YOU WILL BE NEXT!**

Academic Circles

While the exceptional individuals we have examined in earlier sections had to fight for their right to attend universities, possibly beating out other People of Color while pursuing their graduate studies, your professors and supervisors are not barring your entry—hopefully. In fact, most want you there! Most of them understand the importance of diversity in academia. They want to ensure that every one of their scholars has an enriched and fulfilling experience so that they, too, can move into positions of professors and researchers. They want as many people as possible to contribute to the studies to which they have dedicated their lives, and many professors understand that your unique perspective could enrich their field. So while you may feel alone—know this—you are not alone. However, you can build an academic circle to alleviate loneliness if it arises.

One of the most rewarding elements of broadening your educational horizons is the experience. Being exposed to people from all over the world, who have different world views and ways of life, changes your perspective. As you move further into adulthood, the debates and conversations you engage in with different people help you discover more about yourself and others.

Your intellectual growth is heightened in graduate school. For people who go through undergraduate programs in their home towns (nothing wrong with this by the way), attending a graduate school in a different city, state, or country can be the defining moment in your young adult life. A university is one of the few places where the world comes to you. You might have had a few classmates from different parts of the world in your high school. However, graduate school will expose you to hundreds, if not thousands, of international graduate scholars. There will be people who look like you but do not sound like you. There will be people who resemble your high school nemeses who become your best friends. There will be so many different cultures, religions, ideals, and values floating around that—for the first time in your life—you will get to decide what suits you the best. It goes the same for everyone. Everyone exposed to diversity becomes more open, accepting, and broadminded in their approach to academia and life. The only difference, you are all smart enough to recognize it now.

Your prejudices will be challenged. When you drop your biases and witness others do the same, you will feel free to come into your own as a person and academic. This can only happen if there is diversity inside the academic circles that you are a part of. The walls are dropped. The conversations become more honest. Not only this, but you will become more adept at articulating yourself. As a graduate student you will learn to communicate precisely what you mean without beating around the proverbial bush. This encourages the development of thought-processing skills, as you will have to think clearly before you speak knowledgeably.

This new, diverse academic circle will be present amongst faculty members as well. If you really want to uplift more People of Color in academia, then using your degrees to become a professor is one of the best ways to do this, which is why you will meet diverse instructors. However, a professorship is not the only path. As someone who works outside of academia, I know there are a multitude of ways to enrich the lives of others without following the traditional professor track. Nevertheless, if you choose to become one, you will be a positive role model for many of the students in your stead. If so, you will have the opportunity to help another student form their own circle in academia.

Chapter 1

Diverse Universities

People of Color are not just earning professorships; we are running entire universities and launching a few of our own. In this next section, let us examine a few possibilities that you have before you to shed some light on the many avenues available to us in academia.

Historically Black Colleges and Universities (HBCUs), are some of the most diverse institutions in the country. There are over 100 HBCUs in the US, and the boards of these superb institutions understand—better than most—how vital diversity is to higher education. This is true for many, including women, and previously marginalized people, such as the LGBTQ+ community. Their strides toward more inclusive campuses and diversity in their graduate schools make HBCUs some of the best options for a genuinely explorative higher-education experience. They are thriving in the twenty-first century with record-breaking matriculation, and many have graduate programs that are expanding because of it.

There are dozens of female-led universities in the US and hundreds more worldwide. These institutions are filled with students who identify as female, as it gives them all the opportunity to exclude at least one stressor from the higher education experience. Some of them are world-class universities that train future world leaders.

There are hundreds more universities for specific religious preferences, and they offer unique opportunities to learn and fellowship with individuals who share your religious beliefs. They provide communal networks worldwide and the place to practice your religion openly and freely with everyone on campus, including your professors, which gives you an immediate point of connection even if you have no other way of relating to others in your cohort.

Later on in the guide, I will provide you with tips on how to find the right university for you. That being said, you should use your better judgment—and research skills—to make informed decisions for yourself. Research and explore what university suits your personal, professional, and academic goals.

We are steadily moving into an era that is redefining the norm and embracing the vast array of unique qualities that every human being has to offer. Thus, universities that cater to diverse students offer great opportunities for fellowship and connection, while others are slowly expanding resources to ensure all feel welcome on their campuses.

Mental Preparation is Half the Battle

The mental battles are often the hardest to win. You need to mentally prepare for this journey, and your friends and family are key in that respect.

Chapter 1

Preparing for the usual questions from others who need help understanding your choice is vital to your success. You need to be ready for people in your family who cannot comprehend why you are not just looking for a job right after earning your bachelor's like everyone else. You might have a partner or friends who question your decision since their job is so great. People, generally, do not understand the benefits of academic pursuits. For many people, education is something you have to get a job. It is a chore, not a labor of love. For people like you, who love for your field of study and want the accolades that come along with pursuing your dream, nothing could be further from the truth. This is not about a job; this is about fulfilling a burning passion inside of you, while finding a career that lets you explore the subject you love.

You need to understand that two types of people will worry about your decision to enroll in graduate school: those with your best interests at heart and those who wish to see you live a mediocre life. Your task is to figure out the difference between the two.

For most, your parents, guardians, or other loving family members are only concerned about your future career prospects and income. They will be worried about hefty student loans. They will be terrified that you are missing out on the "prime" years to build up work experience for more education. They fear that you will decide to walk away from your studies halfway through once things get too hard. What they do not know is that you have run all of these scenarios through your head a hundred times and no one is more concerned than you are. It is your future after all. Thankfully, with this book you can plan for many of those occurrences before they arise. Be kind with your words for those who genuinely care about you. You will need their support to see you through the challenges you might face during your journey. Let them know AJ is helping you, and even show them the written plan after it is finished.

Ignore those who talk for the sake of talking, or want to hold you back because they cannot see past their own small view of the world. The following section is for people like them. Allowing people to get under your skin will get you worked up. As such, instead of surging ahead with your studies for the love of what you are doing, you might find yourself pushing forward to spite the naysayers. While using negative comments as motivation can work in the short term, it can also cloud your judgment and hurt you mentally in the long run. This should be a journey pursuing something you love, not a journey away from someone you despise. So I want you to ignore the detractors of your happiness as much as possible. Focus on your goals, which we will discuss later, and let love be your guide during this journey.

With that said...

Chapter 1

NFG

I am a Marine after all, and I cannot write a book without cursing in at least one section. The best place is the section I want you to walk away with a motto for graduate school when times get hard, when life as it comes at you with a new challenge, or if someone or something attempts to block your path:

Fuck'em.

When you are the only person who looks like you in your cohort, academic field, or your workplace, you have to form an impenetrable barrier of fuck'em around yourself, one that protects both you and your boundaries. Obstructions will arise during your journey, placed there by others who do not understand you or what you have planned for your life. Some will come from people you know and trust, others from strangers. At times they will look like you, but most of the time they will not. No matter the case, you will walk this path with your fuck'em armor on, and when they try to block out your light you will simply shine brighter just to watch them get upset by it all.

Want to know a secret? Most privileged people grew up with this mentality. When you see a "Karen" and others who seem to not care how they are perceived since they are always correct, it is a sign they were taught early in life to fight for what they thought was right even if everyone else told them they were wrong. That same mentality is why so many privileged individuals stay privileged. They were gifted with money, status, and in some cases, rights that others were not given, and they are willing to do whatever it takes to keep things in their favor. You cannot fight against oppression by playing nice and staying quiet. You need to harness their toxic power for **good**.

As you go through your journey, I want you to keep this motto close to your heart. When someone attempts to block your path: Fuck'em. If an institution rejects your application: Fuck'em. When someone tells you that you are not good enough: Fuck'em. Some racist, sexist, misogynistic, incel attempts to create a roadblock or attack you on your journey: Fuck Them!

I do not give a fuck what arises in your life, do not let anyone or anything stop you from pursuing your path toward your happiness.

*

I know it is hard, but for a moment, I need you to consider why you are good enough to get this done. You have come so far in life. Look back on all of the discomfort, pain, frustration, and sidelining you have overcome up until this point through high school and undergraduate study. You are older, wiser, and can start truly using your voice. Stepping into your superpower means unapologetically standing as you are and walking bravely into academia with the focus placed on your future and nothing else. You cannot pour from an empty cup so focus on filling your cup for this chapter of your life.

Chapter 1

When it is full, you can set your sights on leaving the door open for those coming behind you and empowering others. Your presence in graduate school is more than enough inspiration for now. Just focus on yourself, your mental health, and your future success.

ESTABLISHING A SUPPORT SYSTEM

Establishing a support system early on during your academic career is the equivalent of having a lifeboat in case your proverbial ship goes down. Surviving the mental strain of graduate school alone is extremely difficult. While it is not entirely impossible to move through this chapter of your life alone, having a support system to lean on when you need to decompress is a smart move for future success and mental health.

At the end of the day, no matter how intelligent or capable you are, you are a human being. You have emotional and psychological needs that cannot be satisfied while isolating yourself. Trying to grit your teeth and persevere through the challenging moments will only lead to trauma, emotional scarring, and burnout. A support system is separate from saying fuck'em to the naysayers, as these will be the people who help you fulfill your professional and academic goals.

We are all born with particular needs that must be fulfilled to lead whole, balanced lives. These are more commonly referred to as Maslow's Hierarchy of Needs, and as the name suggests, you cannot achieve fulfillment in the upper quadrants of the hierarchy without achieving completion in the lower levels. Have a look at the hierarchy in this illustration below:

Illustration 1: Maslow's Hierarchy of Needs

It is important to understand what all of this means, and as only some of my readers are sociology or psychology majors, let us unpack this hierarchy. Your physiological needs are your basic needs: food, shelter, and clothing. Your safety needs include personal security and job security. Your love and belonging needs, also known as your intimacy needs, include the need for friendship and a sense of connection. Self-esteem, respect, and recognition fall under esteem needs.

Then there is self-actualization which involves the desire to be the very best version that one can be.

When you enter graduate school, you are going to be pursuing self-actualization. However, reaching the top of that pyramid will take an inordinate amount of work if your safety and need for love are not met. If we break those two tiers of the pyramid down further. Safety includes personal security as well. As a Person of Color in the United States, feeling safe and secure is paramount, but it is not easily achieved. As we are all aware, there is a level of distrust in authority figures. While this will vary from person to person, having the necessary support around you is crucial to feeling personally secure and free from the worry of physical threat. Next are the needs which fall under love and belonging. As human beings, we all long for a sense of belonging. We need to feel connected to those around us and have meaningful relationships—both platonic and romantic—to thrive.

Why have I gone to great lengths describing these needs to you?

Once you understand that your emotional needs are essential to your academic career, you will see how valuable having a support system truly is. One cannot happen without the other being firmly in place. It is not a theory; this is a fact. We need to feel emotionally secure and connected to move up the hierarchy and achieve the height of our respective potential.

Chapter 2

Group Support to See You Through

Establishing a support system prior to graduate school is paramount to your future success. This is even more critical if you are heading to another university for your graduate studies and will be on an unfamiliar campus. It is common to complete a bachelor's degree at one university before pursuing your master's elsewhere. The same can be said for exiting one institution after completing your master's to earn your doctorate. Long story short, you may very well find yourself in completely unfamiliar waters, and with this new territory will come a new set of concerns. Other than concerns about the campus culture or coursework, you might also wonder whether you can establish a new support system where you are headed. As a Person of Color, it might have been daunting to reach out and feel welcomed at your current school, and there will be a lot of concern about leaving this support system behind. Moreover, if you completed your undergraduate degree in your hometown and are now switching cities or states to complete your graduate studies, there is also the issue of leaving longtime friends and family members behind.

This is what I recommend: solidify your support system before you leave. Not everyone can come with you on your journey. That is absolutely true. However, you do not have to cut your old support system off just because you are going somewhere new. Ask any academic—and just about any entrepreneur—what they consider the most imperative element of their success. Many will tell you that it was the relationships they nurtured. If you have relationships with your peers, professors, and supervisors, let them know how much you value their relationship. Voice your concerns about the transition that you will be making. Make an effort to stay in touch. Most importantly, "ask and ye shall receive." Ask for their support and explain why it means so much to you.

Being able to reach out to someone after your first day of classes and having that connection to someone who understands you will alleviate considerable stress and strain. On the days when the workload seems too much to bear or when you have a bit of conflict to contend with, those people who know how you operate around campus will give you insight into the situation. They will help you work through the grind, one day at a time. They will keep you centered and focused on the prize. Having past professors on your team will also open you up to potential connections before you set foot on your new campus. In academia, professors and other academics communicate with one another regularly. Whether through collaboration on a research paper or conducting peer reviews for one another, your professors are in constant communication with others. This could be your window into working with someone who is trusted by someone who you trust. As an added bonus, you will have a recommendation or introduction from someone respected in their field.

We live in the twenty-first century; what does that mean? Digital Age! One of my children is a toddler with a cell phone and tablet. You are likely reading this on a digital device to save money. We all have access to one another because of the digital age, which means you can build a support system worldwide. I may have been the only veteran in my cohort, but the internet was an easy way to connect with dozens more on campus. Thus, it was a great tool to communicate with others before my first day of classes. Even if you are so unique that you cannot find anyone to connect with on campus, the technology available at your fingertips connects you with everyone with the same technology. You could be the only person like you at your university, but guess what? You are not the only one in the whole world. Furthermore, most professors are accessible via the internet on numerous websites, and they enjoy when students contact them with poignant questions as they are always on the lookout for the next great talent. The right email or message could land you a position working with a world-class researcher.

Your support system is not limited to those you already know. I have leaned on people I only know as their avatars or by usernames, and they have been supportive friends along my journey. Social media can be a wonderful place sometimes. Thus, even if you have unsupportive friends, family, or professors, you can always build a support system while still deciding if graduate school is the right place for you. You can continue to build one once you enter, and most importantly, you should continue to create one after you graduate.

Building an academic support system before applying for graduate school will make the decision and transition more manageable. Stepping into a new school without any contacts or support will make you anxious. If you stick to this simple step, you will have a seamless transitory experience that can lead to more productivity and collaboration during your time in grad school.

Leaning on Loved Ones

The relationships that you hold with friends and family are sacred. If you are lucky enough to have a family supporting your decision, you should count your blessings. Some people have toxic family systems that drain and deplete their energy rather than restore it. You also need to look out for this as you move into this next phase of your life, as people can change on you. Dealing with toxic family members can be soul-crushing. As children, we build our identity around a combination of what we are taught, what we are exposed to, and the norms we experience in our households. As we age, especially once we have experienced the mind-broadening effects of college or university, we start to see the world a little differently. In most cases, this is welcomed by our family members and friends. However, in other instances, where toxic relationships and world views are concerned, this is not embraced as readily. You have to decide whether to keep such people in your life or cut the cord.

Chapter 2

The truth is that only you can decide who is toxic to you and who is not. You have to understand the feelings and the energy that certain people in your life give off. You must establish firm boundaries and put your mental health at the forefront of your decisions. You will have to make a personal decision to limit how much you tell toxic family members in your life and how much access they have to you or choose to cut them off completely. Trust your gut, as you know them and yourself. I can, however, provide you with some of the hallmark signs of toxic energy in a friend or family member:

- You feel like they manipulate you into doing things you do not want to do, or attempt to make you feel guilty for following your own path.
- You feel like only they are allowed to voice their opinions while yours is silenced in their presence.
- You feel hurt or confused by their words or actions.
- They constantly belittle you.
- They make you second guess yourself.
- You feel anxious when you know they will be somewhere you are going and when you are around them.
- You are hesitant to tell them about your accolades because you know they will downplay your success.
- They exhibit jealous behavior and speak ill of you or people you care about.

While these are just a handful of the signs of a toxic relationship, this should give you a good indication of who might be draining you more than they are restoring you. Energy does not lie, and you should listen to your own. Remember, **fuck'em** if they are not supportive.

For those loving individuals who only want to help you succeed in life, keep them close. Even if it is just one person, find someone in your family you can lean on now and in the future. Trust me, you will need them down the line. Stay in touch, build the relationship and make it stronger if you can. Tell them how much you need them and how important they are to your future, as loving individuals will typically arise to the challenge. You know your family, and you know yourself. If it is one or thirty, find family members to see you through.

I feel fortunate to have had a rock-solid support system before I began my graduate studies. My wife and children were tremendously supportive of my decision, and they all adjusted their lives to help me along my journey. In professional settings, I often met with my colleagues after work to discuss what a doctorate program was like, and their answers assuaged all my concerns. Dozens of individuals I met over the internet all provided unique stories and solutions as I needed them throughout my journey. With assistance from these three groups, I thrived in graduate school. Because of my support system, I could finish my doctorate in four years, so trust me when I stress the importance of a good one.

For those of you who will be taking a hiatus from work to pursue your studies, there is always the worry that you might be making the wrong decision. What if the job market is not as great when you finish your studies? What if you cannot find another job? What if your savings, grants, or loans are insufficient for living expenses? What will you do for money? How will you survive? If you have children, how are you going to continue providing them with the same lifestyle that they are accustomed to? There are so many questions that will be floating around in your mind. Having someone to talk to—someone with similar responsibilities who answered those questions for themselves—will help you solve many of these issues before they arise. More often than not, a scary thought is only frightening when it is in your head. Once you get it out into the open, it loses its edge, and the right friend will offer an easy answer. Anxiety and worry can be beaten with the right people around you.

If you do not have family members that are mentally or financially supportive, this part of your life will be much harder for you than it is for people who do have that support. Broadening your network before and during graduate school is imperative. You need to mingle with new people, take up a new hobby, or find like-minded individuals who can become your new tribe—your surrogate family. Finding a mentor is also an excellent alternative for anyone in your position because they will provide that older, stoic character you need as a personal guide along your new journey.

Other than family members, you also need to be surrounded by supportive friends. I am not saying you need to have fifty people on speed dial, but a close circle of loving friends who understand you will make this path to success less lonely. The one thing I will ask of you is for you to consider the company you keep. If you do not have friends who can support you, why are they your friends? If you must defend your choices and explain every facet of yourself to people, only to be belittled or misunderstood, those people are not your friends. If they are a toxic friend, then reconsider the relationship, and without the blood tie, they are even easier to remove from your life.

Ultimately, letting go of old relationships can feel like you are losing little pieces of yourself, but those pieces are only making room for the new you—the brave, loved, and supported in everything you do. Build a circle of loved ones who will support you, and they will ensure your academic journey is a smooth one.

Campus Support Team

Creating a support team on campus is equally important. While building strong relationships with your current professors during undergraduate study can help you establish connections with new professors, you should work to create a full support system on whatever campus you intend to attend. Even if you are in the early phases of your university search and decide to attend another university, the peers you meet could one day be your colleagues years down the line. Email professors and student resource centers on campus to seek student support. It does not matter if you are twenty or sixty years old; utilizing the resources available to you on campus is a smart move to ensure you have peers you can commensurate with. Additionally, counselors, advisors, and career coaches are great resources to contact, as their jobs revolve around ensuring your success. They will be an outlet for some of your stress during your time on campus, and they can connect you with groups of students in the same mental or emotional state you are in. You should strive to meet with people you assign to your campus support team regularly. Remember, consulting with them is included in your fees, so why not take full advantage of their services? Feel free to be the person who asks for help and asks a lot of questions. No one will come and give you permission to excel in your academic career, and no one will provide you with the answers you do not seek out. The onus is always going to be on you for your success.

Sometimes, making the first move and introducing yourself to your academic cohort is the best way to meet new people. So many people in your shoes speak of how they built some of the strongest friendships with students in their cohorts simply because they reached out to them. These will become invaluable relationships, especially during the time that you are making your way through graduate school. Few people know the pressure of the program like your peers do. Being able to lean on one another during academically taxing moments and having that camaraderie will significantly boost your studies and self-esteem. Not only this, but your academic cohort will also provide much-needed companionship as most graduate students are researching far away from their families. You will be around each other often during research, study, classes, and campus events, so it makes sense to have healthy relationships with these people. Furthermore, if they are researching in a similar field, there is a likely chance you will work alongside each other—or at least hear of one another—during your later career. Thus, making friends with your peers is beneficial for your short and long-term goals.

Keep it simple. Start with just one local person if you are not the outgoing type. Ask to grab lunch and build on that relationship. They will then be able to introduce you to more people on campus and in the area. By taking that one small step, you will have opened your world up to several other people who can go on to become a solid support network.

While you are at it, seek out students who have graduated—or near graduation. The reason is that they know what it feels like to be in your shoes. They will provide you with insight into their struggles during their studies. They will also give you the extra motivation to keep going. When they move on after graduation day, keeping in touch with them will provide you with a clear understanding of what is expected when you graduate and your career prospects. By engaging with someone who is a few steps ahead of you on the path, you put yourself ahead of the curve. You will always be able to preempt potential problems before they arise because you will witness another person going through them and thriving despite the challenges!

The most crucial element of building a support network on campus is being as open and honest with yourself as you are with others. Be willing to try new things and venture out of your comfort zone. You are heading to graduate school simply for the degree; you are heading there to learn more about yourself and the world around you. Remember, this is to research a subject or field you love, and the best part is that everyone there is doing the same. Foster love and success in each other as you grow and progress, and you will see it pay dividends for you later in your career.

Give as Much as You Get

So, now you have yourself a great support system, and you feel like you are finding your feet in this crazy, new adventure that you are on. But what about the people who support you? Remember, they need support too. As much as you want to be focused on yourself and getting the most out of your time, you also want to be cognizant of whether you are taking more than you are giving. Nobody wants a leech for a friend, and you do not want to become known as one. It is important to speak up and ask for help or a supportive shoulder when you need it, but you also need to reciprocate the support that you receive. Whether by reciprocating the gestures offered to you, giving your notes to others, helping your family when they need you, or paying it forward by helping other students find their way with their academic careers, it is essential to keep replenishing the well that waters the flowerbed of giving.

Offering to assist your professors is a move that is both courteous to them and beneficial to you. You never know where it might lead. If you show enough initiative, you could find yourself in a paid assistant or teaching position, which could offer work experience for your later career. Additionally, this could be a game-changer in terms of your finances, as being a part of the staff guarantees tuition remission. You will see the importance of this in the next section.

Reciprocating support applies just as much to your friends and peers on campus as it does to your support system back home. Checking in with your loved ones, especially if you know they are going through something difficult, goes a long way to maintaining the relationships you had before graduate school. The last thing you want is to return home with your new degree, but you have nobody to celebrate with because you alienated all your old friends and family. A support team is a two-way system; you build each other up and help the group thrive!

Funding Your Academic Career

Financial support is just as important as emotional support, and depending on your walk of life, it may be **the** critical factor in deciding if you can attend graduate school. Finding funding for graduate school is going to be different for everyone. Why? Well, because everyone has different financial situations. If your parents financed your undergraduate degree, are they able or willing to cover your graduate studies? If not, does the university you are considering offer full research funding? Are there grants or scholarships available to you? If so, do you meet the requirements? If you are working, do you intend to continue at your current job and try to juggle your work and studies? Are there student loans available to you? If so, will the interest rates cripple you after graduation, or can you cope with the payments comfortably?

Again, a lot of questions to consider, and ones I remember quite well when I first approached my wife with the prospect of beginning my first master's. However, these are all questions you need to consider in the planning phase.

The top 3 organizations to approach for graduate grants are:

- Your prospective academic institution.
- Government organizations.
- Foundations or groups with a focus on the research that you plan to conduct.

Almost all of these organizations will require you to contribute to their efforts in some way or another. Your academic institution will expect you to contribute to their research the most. However, government organizations and foundations may require you to commit your services to them for a certain period after you graduate or give them exclusive bids on any applications of your research in the future. Most foundations or academic groups that provide grants will require a paper or two and will want you to cite them as a funding source in your dissertation, thesis, or book so others will know they assisted you on your rise to greatness. These are not the only three funding sources for graduate school, but they are the most common. However, find others more suitable for your financial situation and research goals.

Before looking elsewhere for a grant or scholarship, check with your prospective university's finance department to see if the program is partially or fully funded. Most graduate degrees are supported by the university, and you should strive to let someone else pay for your degree as much as possible. Where else can you look if your potential university does not offer funding for the program you have opted for? There may be dozens, if not hundreds, of programs already partnered with that university because they do not offer grants. There are merit-based, need-based, and research-based grants and scholarships, and you can apply for as many as you need to fund a degree or certificate. Ask questions about all prospective outside funding, as this could be a vital factor that affects your future if you take on debt. If the university is adamant that they have no budget for you, you should consider another university. Remember this, the research you plan to complete benefits the university as much as it benefits you. If you become a world-class researcher, they will put you on their landing page as a notable alum and proudly proclaim they trained you. Thus, if they are not willing to help pay for that training, another will.

Chapter 2

For doctorates only, if the university of your choice does not offer funding for a PhD, they have not really accepted you. Sounds confusing, but it is true. Certain institutions might encourage you to seek additional financing from research institutes or federal grants, but a PhD is almost always fully funded. In most cases, fully funded PhD programs require students to pay their dues by teaching a class or assisting a professor during their studies. While working as a teaching assistant (TA) or graduate assistant (GA), you receive a small stipend and tuition remission because you are part of the university staff. That means zero debt, but the compensation is only enough to cover rent in most cities, so you will need grants or some other source to pay for all of your needs. This can become a balancing act if you already have a job and family to care for. Working through graduate school as a TA, GA, or full-time employee is difficult. As someone who did it themselves, I cannot sugarcoat it for you. However, resources and a collaborative campus support system are available for you to tap into. If the stipend is enough, a fully funded PhD program at least allows you to complete your degree debt free. However, there are other avenues for funding that are not part of your university, and if you are a master's student, they may be needed since most universities do not fully fund a terminal master's degree. Most offer none if you are only pursuing a certificate or auditing a few classes.

The simplest way to find a grant or scholarship that is not part of your university is to search the internet, this is the digital age after all. Simply entering "Grants for (insert your field or community)" will yield numerous results. Avoid the ads at the very top of the page and start looking at the organic search results. Contact your academic support system if you are uncertain of an organization's credibility. Speaking to past professors or future professors and peers about funding sources will help you whittle down the results to the legitimate ones. Government grants are the most widely available, and their instructions are always detailed online. However, the government is not the only institution that offers additional funding.

Foundations and groups that are salient to your area of study are excellent resources for funding, and they could lead to future career prospects! Consider this, you receive funding from company x, and they say you have to work for us for two years after you graduate. Now you have a fully paid-for degree, guaranteed employment for two years, and experience in your field. Considering some people graduate with a degree and feel they cannot find a job in their field, an approach like this ensures you have a foot in the door before you step onto campus. Once again, you have to search for these opportunities. I know from experience they are out there, and finding one can put you on the path towards your future career.

I will say this a lot throughout this book, but research, research, research! It will help you so much more down the line.

Chapter 2

*

Establishing a support system is the precursor to developing your goals. When you feel you are emotionally unstable and do not have a sense of connection to anyone around you, your support system will keep you grounded. Hopefully, they will keep you from making decisions that are too rooted in emotion instead of logic. While true that we require emotion in almost everything we do, decisions about graduate school and your career should have a logical outcome that benefits you and your life. Furthermore, leaning on your loved ones and trusted peers for support will help you recalibrate your senses and focus on the path ahead. Ensure your support system includes financial support so you do not graduate saddled with additional debt and bonus points if you find a funding source that pays for your undergraduate degree retroactively.

Remember, you need your support system, and they need you!

DEVELOPING YOUR GOALS

Your goals are the driving force throughout your life. Making a habit of envisioning your future and planning accordingly will alleviate potential stress in your life. If you are unfamiliar with the process, it can be overwhelming to mentally plot out every step of what you deem the pinnacle of success. This is because envisioning a goal without breaking it down into achievable steps is virtually impossible, and realistically imagining all the hurdles you may face without practice is just as hard. However, that practice is needed, or you will miss out on many important details, and the path to your goal will be unclear. If you want to achieve your goals—professional, personal, or academic—you need to be aware of **every inch** of the path ahead of you.

A lesson I learned during my time in the US Marine Corps is that you should always create SMART goals, a template that has been popularized over the years. SMART stands for Specific, Measurable, Achievable, Relevant, and Time-bound. It might sound straightforward, but you need to take each step seriously to avoid finding yourself unprepared for the mental and spiritual strain that is the beast we call graduate school.

Chapter 3

Specific is the first step toward a SMART goal. For your goal to be specific, it has to be precise and in alignment with your vision and values. Now, have a look at an example of non-specific and specific goals:

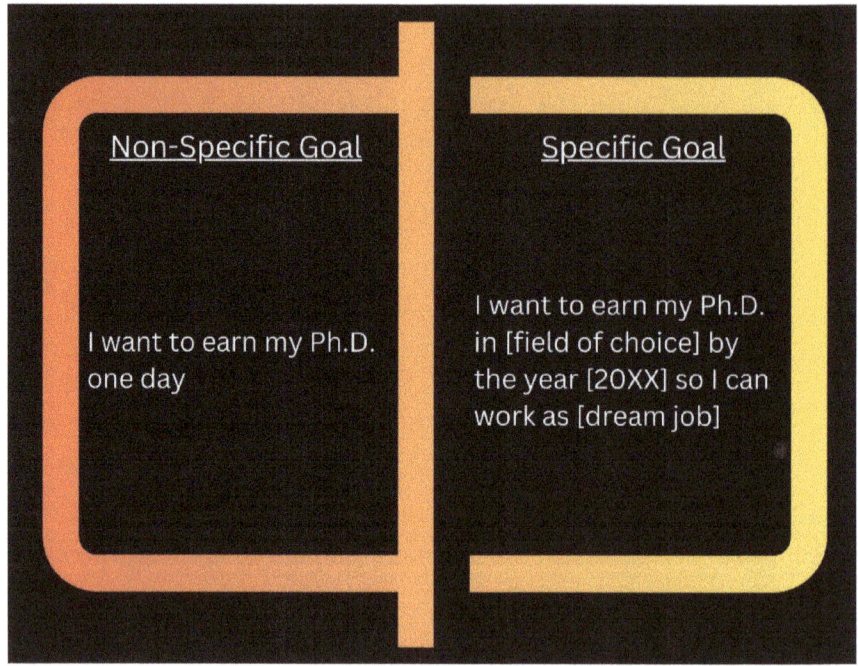

Illustration 2: Non-Specific vs. Specific Goal

Not only have you made your goal specific by using the second approach, but you have also made it time-bound while making it relevant to your life, demonstrating the interconnectivity of the goals.

What does it mean for a goal to be measurable? You can start by jotting down everything you need to do to earn your advanced degree in your specific field. This includes everything from the application processes to acquiring funding and completing your studies. You can then measure or track your progress by dating each milestone you must achieve to earn your graduate degree or certificate. Measure everything, how many credits do you need, when you need them, how much time research and writing will take for your field, and any other relevant measure of time and work you need for your journey. Write it all out for a weekly schedule. Will you have the time and energy? Measure it all. Write it down, print it off, and have someone else read it so they can tell you how achievable it is, as that is the next step.

Are you a high school student hoping to earn your PhD a year after graduating? Are you someone who has worked in your field for several years and hoping to substitute work experience for graduate credits to pursue your PhD? Only one of these situations is viable. Therefore, your goal would only be achievable if you have particular prerequisites. Remember that network of professors you were supposed to form in step one, contact them. Ask them how feasible it is to finish your degree in the time you have allotted. Not to mention, most universities have detailed information on their websites that you can use to compare your plans to what is achievable at that university. If your goal is not achievable, then it is a fantasy, one that will leave you mentally drained once the façade fades in front of your eyes. It is better to have a realistic goal that plays to your strengths before you begin. Once done, you must stick to that plan and work to achieve each objective.

Your goals should be relevant to you, your vision, and your values. Does this desire for an advanced degree align with your life goals? Is it just something you would like to have so people can call you a doctor? Will a graduate degree advance your career or elevate your quality of life? Think about your goal's relevance to your life. Think about the path that you are on and how pursuing this goal will enhance your progress or hinder it. Your short and long-term goals should be relevant to your life's mission. If you plan to be a professor of chemistry, then you should know from the onset what courses you need, the credits for each semester, what internships you should pursue, and who you should work with along the way, all before you even apply to the university. The same is true if you want to be a researcher or start your own business. If your goals are irrelevant to your overall plan, then you should recognize the disconnect and apply elsewhere so you can thrive like I know you can.

Finally, time-bound is the easiest of all these concepts to grasp. While I do not want to pressure you unnecessarily, you must have deadlines for everything. That means setting personal deadlines that might be sooner than even others have selected for you. You need to have deadlines to strategize your day and prioritize your time. Creating time-bound goals keeps you on track because you know how much time you can put toward each milestone. Each step towards your ultimate goal should have a clock, one that you respect. Following those deadlines ensures your future success, and when others intrude on your time, let them know they must respect your progress.

Since we are friends, I will use my PhD journey as an example. When I began, I planned to complete my degree within five years, a tall order for someone working full-time with a family who needed me as well. However, I had some things in my favor, such as a completed master's, which ensured thirty credits on my first day. Nevertheless, my first advisor thought my plan was impossible, so I wrote it in a SMART format. I specified that I would complete my PhD in five years by taking 6 credits every semester for the first two years, as that would put me at my university's threshold to take my comprehensive exams—more on that later. Once done, I would take three to six credits each semester for three more years while I conduct my research. In the interim, I planned to begin research my first semester, so I could start writing by year three. That would give me two to three years to write and edit my final dissertation. Still, they thought it impossible, a folly I am pleased to say I exposed to them. Because I planned adequately from the beginning and stuck to that plan, I completed my doctorate in four years.

Every part of my plan was SMART. I included an Excel spreadsheet with details for each semester (specific). I knew the exact amount of credits I had to take each semester if I planned to graduate in four years (measurable). I even wrote a weekly schedule for coursework and research. I knew I could juggle my work and academic pursuits with the aid of my wife (achievable). I made sure my plan was explicitly detailed to the university I planned to attend, and I knew I needed to maintain my timeline for future career prospects (relevant).

My plan included the overall timeframe and short-term executable goals for each semester (time). I wrote a similar scheme to complete my master's degree in a year. Thus, I can attest that formulating SMART goals before you begin your program lays the foundation for your academic success.

SMART goals are great for your academic and professional life, but you need more for your personal goals.

Developing Your Personal Goals

When developing your personal goals, stop and ask yourself, Am I up for the challenge? (We both know you are) However, knowing what you are and are not willing to take on will help you put things into perspective. If you are at a point where everything is bearing down on you, you might feel like a change of scenery is in order. While that can definitely lead you to new beginnings, it can also put an intense strain on your mental and emotional health. It is important to always weigh the timing and what you can take on at the moment. Putting something off by a year can make a difference in future success. It is better to go into something feeling completely prepared than to walk blindly into a situation just because you are acting on your current emotions. For example, I took a year to mentally prepare and rest between my master's and PhD; that extra year ensured my family and career were in the right place for me to begin. Recognizing how you want to align your personal and professional goals is critical to a healthy balance in your life.

There is also another side to this coin, procrastination. Too many people put things off repeatedly because they do not feel ready. It is important to distinguish between reckless risk-taking and taking a chance on something you genuinely believe in. Plus, if you have done your homework and researched your goal, it is not really taking a chance. Since you are reading a copy of this book, I already know which side of the fence you fall on, but do not let someone else hold you back because of their mindset.

A general rule of thumb, if something consistently comes up in your mind—like a song you cannot get out of your head—then that is a good indication you should consider acting on that idea. If not acted upon, the idea could become a regret later in life. You will wonder what could have been if you had only taken the leap of faith and believed in yourself. Take the time to plan your goals, do as much research as needed, and then **take action**. If you do not, you will find a way of talking yourself out of it or telling yourself that you can always do it a little later. The problem is that tomorrow never comes, and the best time to act will always be now. So if you genuinely love a topic, and you can formulate a SMART goal to research it in graduate school, then go for it!

Developing Your Professional Goals

Similar to personal goals, your professional goals can significantly impact how you approach your academic goals. You are starting to see the evolutionary steps needed to make the most of your graduate studies. It begins with you. It starts with your mentality and your personal goals. When you are disciplined and motivated, understanding your professional goals becomes effortless. You will be clearheaded, and your decisions will be evidence-based, concluded upon sound reasoning. By that same principle, you can develop informed academic goals when your professional goals are clearly mapped out.

The first question you should be asking yourself regarding your professional goals is: Where do I see myself in five years? Cliché, I know, but quite effective. Envision your current career trajectory and see if it lines up with your five-year vision. What steps must you take to bridge the gap between your current position and your future self? While you are at it, consider where you want to be in ten or twenty years. How about forty years? While tomorrow is not promised to anyone, you should plan as if you will be successful for decades to come. You should occasionally envision your **future** and align your **present** to achieve your goals. For example, if you want to be a dentist, what steps must you take today? Knowing that will set the standard.

You can take a few simple steps to create a five-year or ten-year plan. First, evaluate what you want out of life in that timeframe. Next, list the skills and experience that you currently have before comparing them to the skills and experience you need to achieve your plan. Write down the steps you need to take to acquire those skills and that experience level. Then, keep reviewing those steps and your goals. Reach out to your support network, and see what they did along the way. Thousands of successful people gladly write about their actions to success online; go read some in your field and see what they did. Reach out to an idol or mentor and ask them directly what you need to do. There are numerous avenues towards creating SMART professional goals.

You will likely need to major in a specific field of study, write a paper, or papers, on the subject matter, and gain some notoriety as an expert in the field. Do you know what that major or subject might be? Graduate school is different from undergraduate. Chemistry is not a general field when you get to this level; instead, you are studying the chemical reaction of a specific enzyme with precise designs, and your results will be limited, whether successful or not. Do you want to work on that enzyme for the next decade or two? If it will one day cure cancer then I hope so, but these are the questions you need to ask yourself. The same is true for all fields, and the specificity involved means you need to understand your professional goals before planning your academic goals.

It is imperative that you break down your career goals into manageable milestones so that you can see if they will correspond with potential academic goals. For example, if you would like to apply for an executive management position in the next five years, and land the role, consider what qualifications you need. Is a doctorate necessary for this position, or would a master's or an advanced certificate suffice? If so, you could comfortably achieve another five years of work experience alongside a master's in that timeframe. Suppose you have your eye on an academic position such as Dean of a specific school, Head of Department, Vice Chancellor, or Chancellor position; you might need at least a decade of experience in an academic appointment in addition to a PhD. In that case, you could comfortably work toward your master's degree and then your PhD with a solid ten-year plan. However, you want to align these goals with your definition of success.

Ultimately, what you need to do with any goal is to start at the end and work your way backward. Start with the goal in mind and figure out what you need to accomplish before reaching that goal. Then look at what you need to achieve before that and so on. Having an accountability partner at work or in your career field will keep you focused on your goals. Sometimes, just having someone ask how much progress you have made with your goals is enough to make you take stock of how far you have come. My wife was awesome about checking in with me every few months so I could make sure I was on track. If you have made progress, then you will be proud to share the information with them. If you have yet to make much progress, you will be driven to discover why and how you can correct yourself in their eyes (especially if they have eyes like my wife).

I cannot stress enough—you should understand whether or not you need an advanced degree for your potential future career—and, if so, which one you need. If you want a fast and accurate answer to your question, you can start by asking your current employer, professor, or by contacting others in your network. An additional route is a good recruitment website in your field. For example, there are dozens of tech-specific recruiting websites you can browse or contact if that is your field. These sites will provide information on what types of companies are hiring in the specific area you hope to specialize in, giving you insight into potential future employers. You will also get a snapshot of expected remuneration by this year's standards and what would be expected of you in that particular role. Finally, you can preview what qualifications are necessary for that career. This is something to pay attention to because some employers will have hard-set qualification requirements, and others will list specific qualifications as "preferable" for the job. In other words, not mandatory for applicants. However, keep in mind that if they feel comfortable enough to list preferable then that means they have a preferred candidate in mind, and if it is with a company you hope to one-day work with, then you want to make yourself that desired hire.

The next question is, "Can I gain enough noteworthy experience to beat out a qualified contender?" Imagine if a potential employer has two resumes on their screen—one containing your application and one containing another person's—is your experience enough to land you the job if that person has an advanced degree? This all depends on whether you are hoping to rank up in the current company, organization, or institution that you work for or if you are hoping to move on to another company altogether. There are a lot of factors that come into play when you are considering your career prospects. Always weigh the cost of enrolling in graduate school versus the potential benefit of graduating. The cost should always be calculated based on your finances and emotional and mental sacrifices. If you are still uncertain whether you need graduate school to achieve your long-term goals, source a few credible recruitment websites or your network. Once done, you can finally set some academic goals to get there.

Developing Your Academic Goals

It is time to get into the dynamics of a master's compared to a doctorate. This is going to be a very brief overview of the two graduate programs because each one has a dedicated chapter further along. However, you need to know what is required during the goal development phase. To sum it up, an MA will take you about a year or two to complete, and it can open several career prospects for you. A PhD can take anywhere from four years up to a decade to complete and is more commonly suited to people who want to pursue a career in research or academia. Outside of these two degrees, there are hundreds of advanced certifications that you can pursue in graduate school.

In the US, you have two options here. **Option 1:** You can pursue your master's and decide later whether or not you want to pursue your doctorate. **Option 2:** If you are set on pursuing your PhD, some institutions will allow you to enroll in a PhD program with the MA material being built into the PhD program. In most other countries, you must apply for and register in these programs separately, as a master's is seen as a precursor to a doctorate. Other than this, the following table details the core differences between the two:

	MA	PhD
Course Structure	➢ Coursework and class attendance are mandatory and/or a thesis.	➢ 2-5 years of coursework and 2-5 years working on your dissertation.
Course Duration	➢ 1-2 years	➢ 4-10 years
Likely Careers	➢ Careers outside of academia.	➢ Careers in research and academia.

Table 1: Differences Between an MA and PhD

This will vary slightly depending on the university you will be enrolled in as well as your field of study, but this is the general timeline and course structure you can expect. Once again, **RESEARCH!** That will let you know what to expect at your university. Whichever route you plan on taking, I recommend reading the entirety of this book to compare the two, as they are both examined at length.

Maintaining Your Motivation

Maintaining your motivation to stick to your plan is one of the hardest things to do. What if a parent dies during your studies? What if the university takes away your funding? What if a global pandemic begins one year into your studies? These are all plausible scenarios, and there are smaller ones where sometimes you do not feel like getting out of bed because you are tired. Some days you will be up, and some days you will be down, but you will have to do the work nonetheless. Another lesson I learned from my time in the Marines is that putting in the work and pushing through even when you are exhausted is the best way to ensure nothing can stop you. Know that your problems will be there whether or not you finish your coursework. You can take some time off to mourn your loved ones, maybe a bit to adjust to a pandemic, find new funding if lost, but you cannot let life get in the way of your future success. I know there will be times when you just cannot simply power through, and that's ok. This is why your support network is so important early on. Maintaining your motivation throughout this journey is key toward later success. Remind yourself what the goal is, and push towards it every day. Find a balance for your mental health but do not give up!

Rest assured that just about everybody is going through one thing or another. If you open up the floodgates and let your cohort know what you are going through, they might have a story or two to share. I hate to say it, but misery loves company, and sometimes commiseration can take the edge off your problems. Tell yourself that you are not alone in how you feel, which will lighten your load. Even if it is only a pound lighter, that is still better than nothing.

Your New Journey

    Lighten everything around you, from your mood to your lighting, and you will notice a change in your demeanor. Go to the gym, go for a run, maybe a date. A break from it all can help reset the mind. Clean out the area that you use to work and organize your desk. It is far easier to start or continue a project when you have a clean and organized space. Cluttered spaces clutter the mind. A confused mind cannot focus on goal-oriented activities. If this does not work as well as you had hoped and you begin to feel like your home or dorm is stifling, get out and find a new hobby. When your mind loses the ability to keep you motivated, it might be linked to the mundanity of everyday life. Changing things by dabbling in a few new interests or activities will spice things up and wake your brain up. Check out campus notice boards for upcoming events, concerts, musicals, open mic nights, and karaoke evenings. Try something entirely out of the norm for you and invite a friend along for the ride. If they are not available, go ahead on your own. You might make a new friend or two in the process. Find things to get excited about and see you through the natural slumps you are bound to go through. They will serve as great distractions and only sway you away from your work for a short time. For more significant issues such as a death in the family, most universities have programs in place to allow you to take time off if needed but do not let one event deter all of your life plans. As a father, I would hate if my children stopped their journey toward success because I died. I would prefer they dedicated their success to my memory rather than accept mundanity in my name.

Chapter 3

Support others and allow them to support you. Offer a hand and reach out for assistance when it is your turn to be on the receiving end. Do this, and you will find that motivation is easy to maintain. Use your support network before, during, and after your advanced degree, and you will find several ways to sustain motivation throughout. Most importantly, write down all your goals and the steps need to get there before moving on to the next chapter.

*

Keeping your goals at the forefront of your mind, as well as the reasons why you set those goals in the first place, will keep you motivated. This is why I mentioned the importance of having SMART goals that are relevant to your life and that align with your vision and values. If they do not, dropping them and walking away will be far too easy. A conclusion too many find on this journey because of poor planning. Few feelings in this world are worse than feeling like a failure, and I do not want one of my friends feeling that way. Part of achieving your goals and feeling like you are accomplishing your purpose in life is being honest with yourself about what that purpose is and why. Set goals for yourself, not for the world to see. Clap for yourself and be proud of yourself. That is how you stay motivated and continue succeeding in everything you do. When you become your own cheerleader, nothing can stop you!

CHOOSING THE RIGHT UNIVERSITY

Selecting the right university is a painstaking process because there are so many great institutions, as well as bad ones. Knowing your goals in precise detail will make choosing a university effortless. Knowing your personal, professional, and academic goals will give you a clearer picture of what you should major in. If you know what to major in, you can find the best university to help you achieve your full potential in that field. Now, you can enroll in almost any major at most universities, but some will better fit you than others. For instance, heading to a university not close to the coastline to further your studies in marine biology may not give you the best training in your field. You may want to study deep space, but your prospective university does not have access to a deep space telescope. Whatever the case, selecting the right—or wrong—university can influence your entire career.

This is especially important for anyone pursuing a research or academic career. Potential employers are going to want to know where and how you conducted the research for your dissertation. If you were holed up in a desert when you should have been knee-deep in a rock pool, that will not fly. Furthermore, you want to find a university with a good reputation in the specific field you are going into. They could rank as one of the top overall universities in the country, but if the program you enroll in is not top of the crop, that will not serve you well in the future.

It is worth stating that you could be the first person to put a university on the map with your research that is not outside the realm of possibility. You need to weigh the risk of that against your personal and professional goals before you make a selection. Even online universities are improving the quality of their education, but many are not respected enough to make the commitment worth it. Look into one if the time commitment is suitable to your life and career, as some of them offer better education than traditional universities. A clear understanding of your goals will help you determine which university and, thus, which program is right for you. Above all, know yourself and understand what you want from this journey.

Start with Your University & Your Major

As mentioned, you need to look for a university known for your particular major and field. Going with any other institution will open fewer doors for you and your career. The first step, select a field that is related to the topic you are passionate about. Next, list at least a dozen universities in your field, as they will be your foundation going forward.

Numerous universities have majors with similar names and objectives, but not all programs are equal. There are several versions of an MBA alone. Taking the time to thoroughly research each of the programs you are considering will always be your first port of call before selecting the dozen that you feel will suit your journey the best.

Have a look at the steps that you can take:

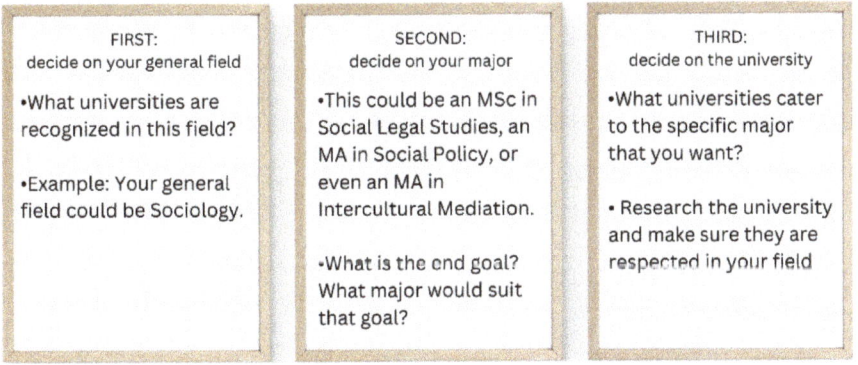

Illustration 3: Deciding on Your University & Major

Before you pick your university, you need to define your goals and find the best program to fit those goals. In most cases, finding the right program will lead you to one clear winner in the battle of the best university for the job. However, there are instances where you will have multiple options that rank closely. Take the dozen universities you think are best suited for your life and begin rating them. It is ok if you do not know much about each at the moment, maybe number one is there because it is where you did your undergraduate studies or a friend is there. The rankings will change as we go through the process.

Chapter 4

Ensuring your program aligns with your career goals is only your first step. Thereafter, you need to assess your personal circumstances. Are you able to commit to a full-time program? Do you require a program that offers you part-time studies so that you can still earn a living? Suppose the program that you choose is only offered as a full-time program at the university. Are you going to miss out on a critical enrichment opportunity for your long-term goals if you go with the next best university that offers part-time programs? These are considerations that should not be taken lightly. The good news is that some full-time programs will be offered in a hybrid environment. This means that you may be able to attend some lectures and submit coursework online. Furthermore, numerous universities offer graduate courses later in the day for working professionals, so you might be able to attend full-time while you work if you are willing to put in the time. This is not a catch-all statement because there are a few fields where it is impossible to have a hybrid environment or research at night; however, if the option exists and you need it then look for the university that suits you best.

Knowing how to research your potential university and preferred major is essential. You need to consider several factors before deciding—the most prominent is the admission requirements. You might be required to go through specific undergraduate coursework to be eligible for your chosen degree. You may have to undergo entrance examinations or show proof of your grade point average (GPA). This not only varies from institution to institution but also from country to country. Understanding where your preferred university is located and all of the implications of studying in that location is paramount. You might want to use the following checklist to establish whether a specific location—whether in another state or another country altogether—is suitable for you.

- What is the currency used in this location?
- Will my funding be provided in that currency or your home currency?
- What is the cost of living near the university?
- Is there affordable and comfortable student accommodation available?
- Is accommodation covered in my funding?
- Do I have the ability to choose off-campus housing?
- Will the stipend cover the cost of housing, and if so, what is the limit?
- Can my spouse and/or children accompany me?
- Are my children of school-going age, and if so, what is the school system like in this area?
- What paperwork will I need to begin preparing to apply for my children to attend a school in this region?
- If I travel abroad, does my student visa allow for spousal accompaniment?
- If staying in my home state, am I missing something by not leaving for another state or country?
- How is this going to positively or negatively impact our family?

Chapter 4

These are all personal questions you need to ask yourself early on in the planning process, and you can answer most of them with simple internet searches and knowing yourself. Look over your list and see which universities remove themselves simply because they do not align with your personal or financial life. If they all pass the mustard then great, but I foresee you having to remove at least two at this point.

> **TOP TIP**: Run a Google search of stores in the area you are planning to move to. Compare staple items such as bread, milk, bottled water, and a preferred protein to gauge how those prices compare to your local prices. Make sure you know the average rent/housing cost. While this will not indicate everything that there is to know about a place, it is a good place to start planning financially.

Other than the tips above, you can also use the table on the following page to map out your university and program preferences. This table is simple enough to replicate as a spreadsheet, and it will give you a side-by-side comparison of your top contenders.

Factor	University 1	University 2	University 3
Research Opportunities			
Institution's Reputation			
Institution's Accreditation			
On-Campus Facilities			
Financial Aid Options			
Duration of Study			

Table 2: Organizing Information on Your Potential Universities

Recreate this table and fill it in with as much detail as possible for your top dozen. Include more rows for your personal and professional goals, and be honest with your assessment of each. It will help you accurately assess your options. From there, you will get into the finer details of admission requirements for each.

The Devil is in the Details

It is time to talk about admission requirements. Read this next part out loud: **research, research, RESEARCH!** All advanced universities want to ensure that you can comprehend instruction which requires you to have a firm grasp of the language in which that particular program will be taught. If you are a citizen of the country where your preferred university is located, this will likely not affect you. However, if you are an international student, you must undergo language proficiency testing, and your transcript will be evaluated by a third party agency that will forward the results to your receiving university to ensure the major was appropriate. To determine whether this is a requirement, you should contact your preferred university's international admissions office and your potential advisor. This process is cumbersome for graduate students who are transferring to an American institution, so be prepared to prove your credits were meaningful. Ensure you have the correct submission forms, as these usually detail all ancillary documents you must attach to your application. In most cases, forms for international students will differ from those offered to local students.

Standard admissions tests that you might come across include:

- **ACT** – American College Testing
- **GMAT** – Graduate Management Admission Test
- **GRE** – Graduate Record Examination
- **TEAS** – Test of Essential Academic Skills
- **LSAT** – Law School Admission Test
- **MCAT** – Medical School Admission Test

As the GMAT and GRE are the most common graduate school admissions tests, we can focus on these. The Graduate Record Examination (GRE) and Graduate Management Admission Test (GMAT) are relatively similar in that they are required for entry to graduate programs. However, GMAT focuses more on business-related fields of study, such as an MBA, while GRE is centered around other general graduate programs that are not independently governed. In that case, you should expect to undergo an MCAT for medical school admissions. Both the GMAT and GRE tests will be made up of verbal reasoning assessments and a written portion of the test. This portion is usually broken down into quantitative and analytical evaluations. More often than not, the university you want to apply to will ask for these scores in the application process. However, do not assume what test you need or the score required for your program. Check the university website or reach out to your network. When in doubt, call the university directly. Do not waste time waiting on an email response for a simple question, as all this research should be completed within a weekend at most.

If you are an international student, you might also be required to undergo language testing. These tests include:

- **IELTS** – International English Language Testing System
- **TOEFL** – Test of English as a Foreign Language
- **DET** – Duolingo English Test
- **PTE** – Pearson English Language Test

One of the testing options above that might surprise you is the Duolingo English Test. You might have seen the app that provides self-learning language lessons advertised on social media. If you did not already know this, Duolingo now

Chapter 4

offers basic English testing, which some institutions accept as proof of language proficiency. No, you cannot submit your language score on the app. You must test in person for Duolingo or any other language test. In the US, the more widely accepted tests are the TOEFL and IELTS. These tests can run up to three hours and include a reading and comprehension portion in addition to listening, speaking, and writing assessments. Again, if you are uncertain about the test you will be expected to undergo, research!

> **TOP TIP:** Several websites offer free practice runs of these tests. Be sure to go through the potential test structure at least once and time yourself while doing so. You do not want to be barred from your future over something as simple as an English Language test.

Language learning was a factor in my decision-making at this point. One of the universities that was number two on my list required their PhD students to be proficient in three languages: English and two others from a pre-selected list. While I can read and speak French and English quite well, I did not want to commit to learning another language that had no impact on my research or career prospects. Thus, I had to remove them even though it was one of my top choices. Honest assessments of your personal, professional, and academic goals will ensure you do not commit to a university or program that offers no benefit or could hinder your future success.

Your New Journey

Another component to be aware of is the time allotted for research and the timetable you have to complete the program. For some of you, having an extended period to work toward your master's or doctorate will benefit your current circumstances. However, there might be those of you who want to complete the program as quickly as possible so that you can move on to the next phase of your development. While there is no right or wrong way to approach that subject, ensure you are not rushing through anything without getting the most out of it. You also need to find out whether or not you have the option to shorten or extend the time it takes for completion. Sometimes, there are set dates of expected completion that cannot be altered. Understanding their time and yours will save you stress in the future.

Finally, it is time to compare all the requirements you have compiled to find a university that is right for you. Make sure that your interests and passions align with the program in question. Review the spreadsheet or document you created and compare the requirements to your professional and academic goals. Now redo that list and see who makes the cut. If you started with a dozen, at least half should be removed at this point because they were outside of your financial requirements, maybe the move is too far, or their requirements are outside of something you are willing to commit to. If you assess each honestly, you will have found six that will not help you thrive in the long run. No matter how much you like the university, program, or professors, if the university does not fit, remove it. The world is full of people who started an advanced degree and stopped because they figured out two years in the program did not work for them. Remember, I want you to thrive, and you cannot do that if you are at a university that will not help you do that. So, trim the fat—no matter how much it hurts—and move on. Once you have removed the bottom six, you should have the top six choices that align with your personal, academic, and professional SMART goals while being a place you can mentally and academically achieve success.

Great news! You just found the six universities you plan to apply to. While your research will detail everything each of your six needs for their applications, most have the following requirements:

- Standardized test scores.
- Transcripts.
- Academic Resume. (tips in a later chapter)
- Two letters of recommendation from past professors.
- A portfolio of research or writing.
- A personal or purpose statement.
- Application fee.
- Transcript evaluation, if you are an international student.

All seem daunting at first, but you should know by now I am not the type of friend to just tell you what you need then walk away. Just be grateful we narrowed your list down, could you imagine doing all of this for a dozen or more universities?

Time to Apply

Navigating the application process does not need to be as stressful as everyone makes it out to be. Being organized and having all the information you need in one folder on your desktop will make for a smooth application process. One academic resume will suffice for each university; you can make a template for your research portfolio and adjust it as needed for each university; letters of recommendation are pretty standard, and most professors have a template they follow; transcripts and test scores will be sent by those organizations; and your university may offer a waiver for their application fee since most undergraduates have economic need as they do not have a job yet. Being prepared for each puts you ahead of the rest, and reminding yourself how prepared you are will calm a lot of your stress.

    Before you begin your application process, it is worth contacting potential advisors or supervisors. Making first contact allows you to establish a relationship with them, and while this is not a technical requirement for admission, it will definitely better your chances. The reason why is graduate students do not simply apply to the university; instead, you are applying to a program to work with a specific professor. Remember that network I told you to establish early on? Time to use them. If not, utilize the power of the internet and search for the professor you plan to work with and send them an email that details who you are, what you study, and how you plan to build on their research. Ask for a meeting if you can—

virtual or in person—and see if you mesh well together. You may find that they are condescending. If so, do you want to work with them for two to eight years? That conversation benefits you as much as it helps them, and if everything seems great then continue with your application. If not, see if you can replace that university with one you cut earlier or limit yourself from six to five applications.

Keep in mind, it is not an automatic "in" just because you emailed a few times with a professor. However, if they see your passion for the subject matter and can tell that you have a good level of knowledge in your field, they will mention this later when everyone in the department is looking over applicants for the next cohort. With that said, keep your communication professional. Do not address them with informal greetings like "Hey" or become overly friendly too quickly. This is not a client or close contact. Use words such as "Hi," "Hello" or even "Dear," followed by the relevant title and name, such as "Dr. XXX" or "Professor XXX." Give them their due respect and ask them about the program that you are considering. Remain professional and talk to them as someone prepared to put in the work to succeed. Maybe even tell them about your professional and academic goals, as it proves you are prepared to succeed. Once they see that passion and professionalism, they will take you as a serious applicant.

While not applicable to all programs, some require an interview before submission. You may be directed to fill out a preliminary application form of intent, and you will receive an interview date thereafter. In some parts of the world, the application process takes place before the academic interview and subsequent submission of ancillary documents that we looked at earlier. Before preparing for this interview, you must know what universities are looking for. Passion is undeniably essential. The admissions officers will want to see your love for the subject. Graduate programs are competitive, and they need to make sure that they admit people who will carry research forward, not people who are just there to add accolades to their resumes or land a job. Having a career in this field and showing how the graduate program would help you excel in this career and add value to the subject in the world is a great way to go about it. However, focus more on what you enjoy about the field of study and what you look forward to achieving at the university. Try to sell them on how you are there to build on the university. If you put in the work I suggested earlier then you should know the answers to all of their questions, and how to phrase those answers to sound as if you are uplifting current research.

Representing yourself as the ideal enrollment candidate is all about correctly choosing your wording. Do not make stuff up for the sake of admission, as it can ruin you if they see through it, and even worse, ruin your career later when you cannot fulfill something you promised if they accept you. Speak your truth at all times, but word it in a light that is positive to the university. This is what you need to keep in mind as you prepare for your academic interview. Remember, the interviewers will only know as much about you as you let on. Keep copies of any documents you submit before the interview, as sometimes they forget to print them off. Go over them repeatedly and ask yourself mock questions in alignment with these documents. Make it clear that you are there for the right reasons. Below are a few questions that you can expect:

- Why did you pick this university?
- What attracted you to this particular program?
- Where do you see yourself in the next five to ten years?
- How would this degree help you get there?
- Tell us about a time you used your undergraduate to add value to your career and the field at large.
- Do you see yourself following the path of academia in the long run?
- Why do you want to work with this professor? If not, then why do you want this degree?
- How will your research benefit our university?

Play the game. Figure out everything there is to know about the university in question, your advisors, and their collective—as well as individual—mission and vision. This will give you ammunition to gear your answers toward those questions. If, for example, a professor is working on collaborative and financial support from a particular organization, tap into this. Mention how you have helped with grant proposals in the past (if you have) and how interested you are in learning more about the principles of sourcing funding to contribute to their research efforts. Use that network of previous professors and ask them what questions you should expect, and if possible, have them interview you first. Watch videos from admission officers and students from that university. Take it from a Marine who survived multiple combat deployments: preparation is vital to success, and you can never be too prepared.

The application process will entail submitting the required information and a series of follow-ups on your application. No, you do not want to be that annoying person constantly blowing up the admissions officers' emails. Still, you want to check in regularly to see if anything has changed regarding the waiting and review period. This year and beyond, you will be expected to fill out an online application that asks for details regarding your personal information, educational background, intended field of study, and all pertinent documents we looked at earlier. Pay attention to all of the details. If you are applying to multiple institutions, set up a spreadsheet that captures the following information:

- ♦ Name of the institution.
- ♦ Name of the graduate program.
- ♦ Responsible advisor or professor.
- ♦ The cut-off date for application.
- ♦ Review period.
- ♦ Expected date of feedback on your application.
- ♦ Contact information.

Chapter 4

Set calendar reminders on both your phone and computer for all of the upcoming important dates, and be sure to check that your application has been received. Even if you submit your application solely online, you need to ensure that the website did not inadvertently crash, thus losing all of your information in the process. If you are mailing in any copies of documents that have been certified by an attorney, you will want to use registered mail so that you can track the package's arrival, and check in with the university once it has been delivered.

After your application is successfully submitted, check in with the university on the date of expected feedback and every week after that if you still have yet to hear back from them. Eventually, you will start to receive some letters, and you will have some decisions to make.

If you followed all of the steps I suggested so far then you are in a good place, but I have some bad news: you will **not** be accepted to all of them. The most common reason someone is rejected is they did not meet the minimum qualifications or were just slightly over, and in a competitive program, another candidate having a higher test score or GPA can make a huge difference when decisions have to be made. Even if you are a top-tier candidate, there could be another who is coming in that tops you. Perhaps the professor you want to work with is taking a sabbatical, so they are not taking any new students this year. There have even been cases of universities closing entire departments because of financial constraints. Whatever the case, remember that Germany lost Einstein and that university just lost you. Rejection is why I want you to apply to six universities. It gives you a breadth of choices, and even if three reject you, three will accept you. If you only applied to three and it was the wrong three, then you would have received only rejection letters and thought you were not good enough. If all six accept you, wonderful; if only one does, that is still fantastic news.

Now it is the university's time to sell you on them. Reach out to each that accepted you, thank them for their time, and then reach out to your potential advisor and let them know you need to meet again as it is decision time.

Academic Advisors: An Underutilized Resource

Before selecting the winning university, contact the advisors responsible for your field of study. Let them know you were accepted to their university, but also let them know you were admitted to others. Academics are less competitive than you may think, and most will be open to the idea of selling you on their program. If you receive an abrupt or angry response, well, they may have just saved you the trouble of working with a professor with untreated anger issues. Be grateful they were obvious about it and move on.

Remember this, graduate school is where things get more involved. You will be contributing to your field and might need to join a specific professor's team to accomplish this. You will be working with them for years, and depending on the field, you may work with them for decades after earning your degree. There was one person I chose not to work with—through no fault of his own—and we have seen each other at numerous conferences and events over the years. Thankfully, he understood my choice, and our conversations were always cordial.

Meet with all your potential advisors for each university that accepts you, even if you are a year away from enrollment, as it is never too early to start forming a relationship with the key player in your future academic success. Find out more about what they look for in a graduate student and learn as much as you can about their research. This is your opportunity to interview them, as you have options now. Look for angles to form your thesis or dissertation proposal and how their research will help your future compared to others. They know you are there to develop a mutually beneficial relationship, and if this second meeting demonstrates you two cannot do that then save yourself the trouble. You also want to get a feel for your potential advisor's personality. This is essentially going to be your mentor. If you have a few differences in opinion that is one thing, but if you do not get along at all, that will be a tricky situation. With that being said, if the advisor is not a good fit but the program is, see if there is another professor you could potentially work with. I had a falling out with my original advisor two years into my doctorate, and my new one was great. I was able to keep everything on track with only a few days of research lost, so do not feel as if you are tethered to this person, but you do want to be selective as possible before you decide on the university.

The final stop on your list will be identifying the university culture. Visit the campus and meet with students before making your final decision. What is the atmosphere like? Do you feel at home here? Do you feel welcome? Can you see yourself spending most of your day here for the next few years? Do you feel safe or out of place as a Person of Color on campus? I cannot stress the importance of these questions. There is no point in being somewhere that is going to make you feel miserable and add extra weight on your shoulders. Anxiety can play a part in making you feel out of place, but if you are feeling more afraid than you are excited, trust your gut. You want an atmosphere conducive to relationship building, collaboration, and learning.

Decision Time!

Be prepared, as this next step is challenging. Return to your professional and academic goals, compare that to the universities you were accepted to, and start making cuts. This is the time that any minute detail means they are removed. Not enough of a stipend? Cut! Professor was curt for no reason? Cut! They want you to learn three languages that will never help your career? Cut! Is your gut telling you not to trust them? Cut!

Chapter 4

    If you still have two or three that are too hard to decide between then be petty and compare rankings. Which one is more likely to land you a prestigious career afterward? Which one is more respected in the field? Which one made you feel more welcome? Ask your previous professors, and see which one they wish they could have attended. The cream will always rise to the top, and whomever that is becomes your top choice.

    Now that you have finally selected your favorite, all universities have a formal process for you to inform them. You want to first accept your top choice formally, and then informally inform your future advisor through email you will be joining them soon. Next, you must go back and formally decline all your other options. Remain professional and cordial with all your correspondence. Academia is small, and your field is even smaller. Professors talk, and if you become known as a problem candidate before you even begin your selected university, they could always withdraw your acceptance. Let each professor you turned down know how much you appreciated their willingness to work with you but that you selected another university. You do not need to tell them why, as that could come off as selfish, so phrase it as if it was to benefit them. If you maintain professionalism well enough, you might retain friendships that could help you later in your career.

*

    It is absolutely vital that you pick the right university, as well as the right major, to suit your goals. Several majors might seem like a good fit based on their name and objectives, but taking the time to find out more about each of them will save you a lot of heartache in the long run. Do not underestimate the value of academic advisors. It does not matter if you are twenty or eighty years old. Having the mindset of the "forever learner" and asking questions before making assumptions is crucial to any field of study. Do your due diligence and make wise choices. While it is never too late to go back and get an advanced degree in another major, not all of us have the time or resources to do that. Make sure you are making the right decisions early on, and you will thank yourself for it later. Be selective in which universities you apply to and even more so for which one you accept. The university you attend will influence your career for the rest of your life.

STARTING GRADUATE SCHOOL

Now, we are going to be talking about the part that has had everyone on the edge of their seats: starting graduate school and the variety of emotions that come with those first couple of days on campus. You will be excited, apprehensive, anxious, overjoyed, and maybe a little intimidated by the colossal task you have just taken on. Even if you are like me and the only person who looks like you in the entire cohort, remind yourself they probably feel the same way you do. It is all normal. Know that everyone goes through these jitters and that you are ready. Most importantly, know that you deserve to be there!

While everything is new and crazy, remember you chose this and planned everything out months in advance. The SMART goals you created mean you already know what you need to do each semester, when you plan to graduate, and what you plan to do with your degree once you have it. So, there is no need to freak out as you are ready to thrive on your new journey. However, there are some key points you need to prepare for along that journey to ensure you succeed day to day.

Operating Expenses

Beginning this leg of your journey fully prepared is vital. Let us start by considering your finances and budgeting accordingly.

Financial constraints will rattle just about anybody, so having your ducks in a row will take the edge off. If you are relying solely on the funding provided via the department, it is time to get clever with it. If you have any additional sources of income, such as working your current job while studying part-time or studying full-time with a modest savings account, add this to the total funding you will receive. Usually, you will be provided with a portion of your total funding at regular intervals. This will either be at the beginning of the academic year or at the beginning of each semester. If you will be receiving a portion of your funding each semester, divide that by the number of months you have until the next semester and spend it as if you are being paid monthly. If you are currently employed, add this to your monthly funding figure and determine the best way to budget this money. If you will not be working during the time that you are in grad school, but you have some money set aside for this particular time in your life, add that to the total funding amount and divide that sum by the number of months that you expect to take to complete the program. Always overshoot this number. Anything can come up, and if your program allows you to, you might need to prolong the time you take to complete the program.

Chapter 5

Once you have done this, start working on your monthly budget. Ideally, you want to use what is known as a zero-based budget. This is where you would give every single dollar that you have per month somewhere to go, leaving you with a zero-dollar figure at the end of each month. Now, this does not mean you will spend every dollar you have to your name. However, it does mean you need to label every dollar and give it a job. Once you have covered all of your basic expenses, divide whatever is left over into categories such as:

- ♦ Emergency fund.
- ♦ Car fund.
- ♦ Unforeseen expenditure.
- ♦ Entertainment fund (hobbies and activities).

These are just a few examples to get you started. If you have a pet, consider an emergency fund for them. If you do not have a vehicle but plan on saving for one, you could start a savings fund. Budgeting your money this way ensures that you stick to a monthly routine and always have other pots to dip into if there is ever an emergency. Look at your funding and expenses the way a business would. You want to keep yourself in the black to avoid graduating with unregulated debt that you could have easily avoided if you planned early. If you cannot do all of this on your own, there are numerous budgeting apps and tools that can help you maintain your finances during your studies.

A Plan for Every Year

Creating a general plan of action before you begin is advisable. This should cover everything from your potential timetable to the time you will set aside for personal review. This time will be used to assess whether or not you are on track with your goals. Try to set targets for each semester. What connections do you want to make? Are there potential employers or organizations you want to start linking with? If you are fresh out of an undergrad program, you will be pleased to notice that your workload will lean more toward research and writing and less toward physical classes. That extra time should be used for study or preparation for your future success. Connect with prospective employers, work on a paper for publication, find an internship, go to academic conferences, join the appropriate societies that can aid your career, and if you do not know what will help, speak with your advisor as it is their job to advise you.

When it comes to time management, using something practical, such as the Pomodoro Technique, will allow you to easily manage your time efficiently and work through your coursework. What is the Pomodoro Technique, you ask? Well, it is a time-blocking technique that allows you to have an unwavering focus on one task for specific periods of time. While many of us think we are great at multitasking, most are not. In fact, only about 2.5% of the general population can multitask efficiently. For the rest of you, juggling work makes you less productive.

Chapter 5

To use this technique—whether you are planning your day or knocking out a few tasks—you need to get your phone out and set a timer for thirty minutes. During that time, focus entirely on one task. Ignore calls and emails, only responding to them once the timer is up. Obviously, if someone in your immediate circle is calling, it might be urgent; however, if not, mention that you are working now and call back later. For those you care about, give them a predetermined code word to text you if something needs your urgent attention. After that, it is back to work until the time is up. Once done, stop what you are doing and take a ten-minute break. You will come back feeling recharged and ready to complete the task in the next block on your agenda. Repeat this process throughout the day, and you will find that you have time for social media, friends, and work without interfering with one another.

Working in this manner will empower you to stick to your plans. Be sure to review those plans every semester, as mentioned, to see if you are on track. Constantly remind yourself of your goals and what drives you. Check back in with your advisors and support system to keep you afloat, and you will find this phase of your life is practically effortless. When you have plans and checklists in place, you reduce your mental load tremendously as you will not have to continually think about what to do next or what you are missing.

Time management is absolutely essential. If you are prone to procrastinating or putting things off just because you do not have to finish them right that minute, you are in for a world of hurt. Prioritize every minute of your day and try to work smarter, not harder. Getting into a rhythm with your weekly schedule will be challenging initially, but you must do this. Time-blocking is going to have to become a priority. Have specific days for replying to emails, conducting research, working collaboratively, and spending quality time with your loved ones. There has to be a day for everything, and you have to be vigilant in not letting one-day bleed over into the next.

Most importantly, you need to schedule a block of **time for yourself!** Time for the gym, video games, sleep, or simply watching crappy TV is just as important as your research. This is the only way to maintain a healthy work/study/life balance. Do not try to take on too much. Delegate when you have to and ask for help when you feel like you are drowning.

Roll Call!

Going to class during grad school is more important than your undergraduate years. You have to be attentive and immerse yourself in what is being taught. You will also find that these classes are more discussion-based, and your professors are there to facilitate collaboration amongst you and your peers while inspiring further passion in the subject matter. If you have not experienced this during your undergraduate study, you will begin to notice how attending classes will help you absorb the material more readily than just trying to read over the coursework on your own.

Chapter 5

If you recall, I mentioned how human beings have been storytellers since time immemorial. We learn much faster when we feel like we are part of the story or conversation, which is precisely the feeling that attending graduate-level classes elicits. Otherwise, if you constantly miss classes, your professors will not take you seriously. If you are working toward your master's and hoping to move on to your doctorate at the same institution, you can kiss that dream goodbye. If you are a PhD student, they can drop you from the program to let in someone on the waitlist. Even if you decide to pursue your PhD elsewhere, you will need those professors who dropped you to write a letter of recommendation. So, to avoid that hassle, put your best foot forward and take your future seriously by attending all your classes. If you do not have the passion for the classes, then you will not have it for the subject matter. If it seems that terrible, reevaluate your choices and save yourself before you are in a career you hate.

Why else is class attendance so important? Well, these are the years when you can take notes and use your critical thinking skills to form ideas. Engaging in conversation during lectures can ignite a "brain spark" that you might not have the answer to right now. These are notes that you should hold onto for years. Digitize them and take them wherever you go. If you do this, that brain spark might turn into a breakthrough a few years later. During graduate school, these notes will provide helpful hints to come back to when it is time to start preparing for comprehensive examinations. Your professors are not just going to be throwing random information at you.

They will provide you with all the information you need to tackle those examinations. Moreover, research shows that people who attend classes and engage with their professors during office hours tend to produce better results and earn higher grades. Take advantage of every moment you have to pick your professors' brains. They earned that position, and most know what they are doing.

That brings me to my next point. Engaging with everyone around you is going to work to your benefit. Not only are your professors an important resource. Your peers are too! You are all important to one another as you are all pieces of the bigger puzzle. Bounce ideas off one another. Have light-hearted discussions and intense debates. Allow yourself to see things from another person's perspective and give them your own. Other than professors and peers, there are also peer educators. If you do not find yourself in a teaching or assistant position during your first year of graduate school, you might make your way there in your second year. Engaging with current peer educators or assistants will provide you with a different level of emotional support and insider insight on landing a position of that nature if that is part of your long-term plan. The fact that they understand what you are experiencing will make them that much more receptive to you and your requests.

If you are unable to find anyone to connect with because you feel out of place, there are options out there. First, speak to someone. Search social media and find someone off campus to connect with. Maybe look in your university's local community, and you might find a friend. You can also speak with the person who made you feel out of place. It may be a misunderstanding or something your professors can fix. Maybe they did not know your religious beliefs made you feel ostracized; perhaps your culture has a different meaning to a phrase they commonly use; or maybe a few of your peers did not recognize their macroaggressions because they have never been around people with diverse backgrounds. Speaking up is the first step toward resolving an issue. If it was purposeful, well fuck'em then. Second, use social media and find others you can connect with. There may be others who feel as you do, and you can form a support group online like I did. Third, file a complaint if it is warranted. Most universities operate as businesses, and you are the customer. If you file a complaint about something, typically, they will work to rectify the situation. However, at the end of the day, you cannot let others in your department affect your future. You must go to class, engage in research, and be a part of the discussion if you are going to succeed. Find people to connect with as you cannot complete this journey alone.

An Imposter is Among Us

Imposter Syndrome: the beast we all must slay. Imposter syndrome is the feeling that you do not belong somewhere or that you are a fraud. It is this sneaky, little voice in the back of your mind that tells you that it is only a matter of time before everyone else realizes you do not belong there. Nearly all People of Color in graduate programs hear this voice screaming on day one. The worst part, the higher you climb in your field the louder this voice becomes. Weirdly enough, imposter syndrome does not happen to your average person. It primarily affects high achievers—like you—who feel like they are unworthy of their success or accomplishments. People who are incompetent or lack understanding about how vast a subject can be, think they are experts from an internet search. While you will learn how deep the well can go on your topic. Not to mention that the media tends to depict academics as older white men who come from generations of wealth and intellect. If you close your eyes and think about it, I bet you can imagine him in his tweed vest, bowtie, glasses, and massive house with thousands of books. However, I have some news for you: that is total bullshit. In truth, academics can look and sound like anyone willing to do the work. Yes, you read that right: it is not a matter of born intelligence, it is a matter of work ethic. I already know you are willing to put in the work because you purchased this book to prepare yourself.

Nearly everyone in academia experiences imposter syndrome—even that old white professor you met on campus. Like them, you must learn to silence that voice and assure yourself that you are not an imposter. Remember that the department already proved to you they think you are worthy. The people who approved your application are tenured professors, a few might even be world-renowned experts in their field, and **they accepted you**! They are the ones who said you were good enough, not your friends or family, whom you can mentally justify as encouraging you because they are nice. If experts in your field agree you are good enough, then it is safe to assume you are not an imposter. Believe in yourself, your future colleagues already told you they do, so at least listen to them.

However, there is that elephant in the room that makes it difficult. There is a nasty little archetype that the world has seemed to spin that the "tokenization" of People of Color is prevalent in academic circles. You can easily replace color with religious beliefs, sexual orientation, gender, nationality, disability, or any number of examples that made you feel like you would be an outlier when you found this work. However, that is not true for most academic institutions. Because most graduate degree-granting universities are on liberal arts campuses, typically there is already a diverse populace, and there is no need to have a quota for any one group as they all apply anyway.

I can use myself as an example. Living in the Washington, DC area, do you think I was the only African American man to apply for a PhD? Even if they judged me on my race, I can guarantee they had to screen my application against dozens, if not hundreds, of others of the same race. The same is true for you. You earned your place at that university: you made a plan; you followed all of the steps to that plan; and you executed it perfectly. You deserve it and there are no two ways about that! They recognize greatness in you, which is the only reason you are there. Do not allow negative chatter to seep into your mind and muddy your thoughts. Do not let it drive doubt in your heart and make you feel inferior. You are worthy of every single thing you have achieved and are about to achieve. Erase the narrative of it being easy to come up when you are the only one who looks like you in the room, and if a student, professor, or coworker attempts to make you feel that way then prove to them how wrong they are as you surpass them, thinking fuck'em the whole time.

Even if you are not the only Person of Color in the cohort, you will eventually experience imposter syndrome. Even in HBCUs, universities with diverse populations, or a university where everyone has the same faith. Students and professors alike will experience the same emotions because high achievers are perfectionists by nature. However, living with imposter syndrome for prolonged periods can lead to adverse health effects—both psychological and physical. You have to find a way to alleviate the strain this will put you under, and I have a few tips for this too:

- ♦ Talk to yourself like you would speak to a friend if they were going through these emotions.
- ♦ Speak with people outside of your academic circle about your feelings.
- ♦ Release yourself from the need to be perfect at everything.

- Relish in your mistakes and take them as necessary learning curves. Yes, you really can learn from your mistakes!
- Share your mistakes with others, and you will find that many people have similar experiences. This will show you how everyone around you is imperfect and quell the feelings of being an imposter.
- Talk to someone who is not an academic about your research. Sometimes speaking to a novice reminds you of the level of expertise you really have.
- Most importantly, always keep your "why" in mind and develop as much self-compassion for yourself as you would for a close friend or family member if they were in your shoes.

These are only a few tips, and I implore you to look for more that work for you. Imposter syndrome is a beast that will track you wherever you go if you do not find innovative ways to slay it. Although sometimes the beast becomes a zombie; go for the head next time and try again. Find the method that works best for you, because you and I already know you are more than worthy.

The most important thing to keep in mind when dealing with this beast is that you are in graduate school to learn. There is often this belief that you should already know everything or that new information should come easily as it did when you were in high school or even undergraduate. However, you will start graduate school as a neophyte, and you are there to learn like everyone else. A piece of advice I hammer into my children: intelligence is the **ability to learn**, not that you already know it all. Think of people like Albert Einstein, Marie Curie, or Neil deGrasse Tyson. None of them were born knowing their fields. They all went to various schools and universities to learn before they changed the world, and you are following a similar path. If you are willing to do the work, just like they did, you too can thrive!

The Backbone of Graduate Study

The support system I told you about a few chapters ago is essential for graduate students as they will ensure you succeed. Having them as you experience the highs and lows of that first year will get you through the toughest moments. The path you are about to embark upon is not going to be easy, which is why a strong support network of mentors and peers is vital to success. Even with support, forming a battle rhythm will still take some time. For some, a few weeks; for others, a few semesters. Remember that your support system is always there for however long it takes you to find your footing.

Lean on peer educators for advice regarding the program and your upcoming exams. Lean on your advisors for guidance in terms of your career prospects. Lean on your peers for moral support and to share in each other's plights. Lean on your friends and family for emotional support and to just laugh or cry. Reach out to others through social media;

numerous academic circles are open to new researchers experiencing the same first year that you are.

I cannot stress this enough, but I mean it when I say reach out to others. Academia, by design, is a lonely road. Even if you work in a lab or with a team of researchers, the point of academic research is to foster independence. While this is something that is honed with time, if you do not seek others to help you then you will feel overwhelmed, and that beast we spoke of before will come roaring out. Not to mention, as a Person of Color you will feel alone in enough academic circles without you contributing to it. Do not deprive yourself of support by thinking you must become instantly independent just because you are a researcher. Take the time to build a strong backbone group that will support you throughout the rest of your career.

Let Off Some Steam

Finding an outlet while you are in graduate school is of the utmost importance. If you recall, I love working out and animals. After some convincing, I was able to get two dogs running around my house who are great for at-home relaxation, and I go to the gym four to six times a week as well. The combination of the two was fantastic for de-stressing me between work and school. Additionally, hobbies are a great way to ask a peer to join you and build new relationships. Do not underestimate the positive impact of hobbies and new connections on your academic success.

Hitting the gym has lots of great benefits. Other than the obvious ones, such as maintaining good mental and physical health, it also works wonders for your ability to handle pressure. Regular exercise gives you a steadier heart rate and the ability to control your breathing under physical or mental strain. The release of endorphins works great when life has you down, and exercise also helps with maintaining a healthy sex drive. Similar to exercise, sex releases numerous hormones which alleviate stress. Together, the two can aid in managing your emotions as graduate school can weigh heavily on your mind.

There are several other avenues to de-stress and declutter your mind after a long day of research, and if my favorite two do not work for you then find what does. Ride a bike through breezy, sunny streets to and from campus. Play video games with friends or with a virtual team. Cook, sing, dance, or visit a farmer's market. Just find something that brings you joy and lights you up when life attempts to bring you down. Find something you can completely immerse yourself in, where you will not think about research or classes. Dive headfirst into anything that makes you feel alive and revitalized.

Similarly, pick a day to **relax** and make it **sacred**. If you are religious, you should already have a readymade day; if not, create your own. Pick one day—one whole day—in the week where you engage in your soul-nourishing activity. If you think that is too much, consider: I am asking you to take four days off a month. It is too easy to fall into the trap of working hard all day every day as a graduate student, but since you are prepared to work and relax, you will avoid it. Live a little! Let yourself be present in the very moment that you find yourself in. If you love video games, then I want you to play video games all day like a teenager again. If you have a significant other, then it is date day. Have kids like me? Then it is family time all day long. Being present in whatever you do on your days off is just as important as researching because it resets your mind and you return with renewed vigor. More importantly, it gives you something to look forward to. If you are mentally down on a Wednesday but know Saturday is your day off from everything, you can push through until then. This sacred day is needed for mental health, and if anyone asks you to do something on the day, let them know you are busy.

When your thoughts are hard to reign in, you will find it difficult to focus on any task before you. If you push your mental health past its breaking point, it can take years to return from that. Yes—**years**—not weeks, to recover from burnout, as well as all of the physical and mental side effects that come along with it. Skip to the later chapters if you need more tips on avoiding burnout, or ask your emotionally healthy friends and family what they do to maintain work/life balance. Taking the time to relax is essential for maintaining yourself through graduate school and your later career. Relaxation can also give you an aerial view of your life and help assess if what you are stressing over is even worth it. Remind yourself of the adversity you overcame in your past.

You could reaffirm your strength to yourself and resurrect the belief that you can move through any obstacle that comes your way. If things are really bad, move the date up to take a break and breathe.

The worst thing you could do is try to work through a moment of deep distress. Sometimes, putting your head down and working through it will be called for, but if your body is begging you to slow down, listen. Graduate school is a marathon, not a sprint, so take your time and enjoy it.

Find inspiration in the little things and allow yourself the space and grace to experience your life as it happens. There is so much to be grateful for amongst the stressors of daily life. Finding a hobby or activity that is all yours will give you the emotional stability to tap into that attitude of gratitude. All work and no play would make just about anybody feel worn out and moody. You do not need to strive for perfection. You just have to put your best foot forward and cut yourself some slack when necessary.

*

That first year of grad school will be one of the best and most stressful years of your life. Making the most of your time on campus and attending every lecture is going to be an absolute must, but you will enjoy it so much more than your undergraduate classes. Classes are smaller and more in line with your true passion. If you take those classes seriously, you will have little to worry about. Remember to keep tapping into

Chapter 5

your support system at this time. They are relationships that you will have worked hard to nurture and will be a lifeline. Do not forget to let off some steam at the end of the day and to have at least one day a week you take a break. You are only human, after all. Having something fun to look forward to will keep you energized, so do not underestimate the value of finding a great hobby or group activity to enjoy throughout your life.

GETTING YOUR MASTER'S

Some people spend years stuck in neutral—unable to take the first step toward earning their master's degree. Oftentimes, this is due to the belief that the process is too complicated or they are not intelligent enough. There is this idea among many People of Color that a graduate program is an "invite-only" club, and the mere thought of being on campus can make you anxious. On top of that, you might wonder whether you have the necessary knowledge and skill to keep up with the program.

The reality is a master's degree is not about intellect or who you know; it is about effort, so you got this!

While no two programs are alike, there are some general similarities regarding difficulty and length. This difficulty, however, has more to do with you than it has to do with the program itself. If, for example, you will be heading to a graduate program in the fall semester after completing an undergraduate program, you might find that your master's is a little easier in terms of the demand on your schedule. There are fewer classes, and most of your work will be self-directed or independent. Additionally, there are no more general education courses, as every course you take at the graduate level is focused on your degree.

If, on the other hand, you had a hiatus from school and have been in the working world for a couple of years, acclimating to university life may take a while. Additionally, there are the demands of the program in question. Depending on what and where you are studying, you might either thrive with the workload or buckle under it. As with almost anything in life, it is all relative to you, which is why I want you to frontload so much of your planning before you reach this point. If you took the precautions I warned you about earlier, then you will be fully prepared for many—if not all—of the bumps that can arise and you will thrive.

Quick overview, earning your master's degree is primarily class attendance until you reach 30 to 45 credits, depending on your field. All of the courses are self-selected and directed toward your major and nothing else. Every person in your class will be a graduate student or, in some rare cases, an advanced undergraduate. The best part is they all love the subject as much as you. Some universities even have programs that allow you to complete your master's near the same time you earn your bachelor's, so look to see if that option is available. For some, a master's is a terminal degree; for others, it is a stepping stone toward a doctorate. The best part, a master's degree has a choose your adventure option for completing it, so you can dictate how you want to finish in most cases.

Paths to Graduation

Most universities offer two options for completing a master's degree: writing a thesis or completing an exam or series of exams, typically called the test-out option. As the names suggest, in one you write a master's level thesis that contributes to your field in a substantive way for graduation. The other, you complete either one or a series of exams demonstrating mastery of your major. Either option earns you the same degree, but they do have key differences for scientific advancement and career options, so weigh your options carefully and **research** which is best for your field.

The test-out option, sometimes referred to as a taught program in universities outside the US, focuses on examinations after you have completed all of the required credits. The point of the test is to demonstrate your complete mastery of the subject, and your professors will be the ones who administer the test. It can be written, oral, or both, and you will still be expected to conduct some form of research in this program, which can include creating a new learning module, completing an internship, or leading a research project that is not as voluminous as a thesis. However, the focus will be more on class attendance and testing. For those of you who are accustomed to the work environment of an undergraduate program, this will be similar in nature. Some people feel this is the easier option, but this is not true for everyone. While attending classes and undergoing assessments might be the more straightforward, someone else might feel that working on a research project is more manageable. It depends on your learning style and your work methodologies.

> **SIDE NOTE:** Everyone has different learning styles. Some people learn better by conversing with others. Some learn better by reading or watching videos. Some even learn better by listening to lectures. While some even prefer virtual learning. **Know yourself!**

One of the benefits of being in a taught or tested program is you get to engage more with your peers and your professors. Because you will be on campus regularly, it will help you get out of your shell and socialize with others. This option can sometimes be a little costlier than a research-based program, so keep this in mind. Also, be aware that you might have less flexibility with your schedule than with a research-based program. If you need that sense of structure to stay on track, this could be a great option. However, a research program would be ideal if you already have a demanding work-life schedule and believe you can fit your research work in between everything.

Preparing for your exam is a collaborative process as it is not as research intensive, and it is an excellent option for anyone wanting to step into the workforce right after they earn their degree. Thus, it is the option used most often in terminal degrees. You may find that your field does not expect people to earn a doctorate unless they want to teach, so if that is not your career goal, do not waste your time pursuing useless accreditation. If you properly researched your career goals then you will already know what is expected in your field in terms of degree and the preferred graduation option, so you will know from day one what is needed. Remember, preparation is your key to success, so being prepared from the beginning means you will be working towards the end goal while others are still trying to figure out what is going on.

Degree by thesis—also referred to as a research program—is perfect for people who get their best learning done in front of a book (or tablet). If you can absorb vast amounts of knowledge by simply reading and researching the topics by yourself then this is a good option. Keep in mind that if you want to pursue a career in academics or go on to earn your doctorate, this would be the more advisable route to take. Most liberal arts degrees prefer the thesis option, as it demonstrates your ability to research, write, and produce content. However, more STEM-related fields are pushing for a thesis, and even engineers are expected to think and write critically in the modern age. The reason, a thesis requires a commitment to one area of expertise in your field of study, and writing a thesis cements you as an authority on that subject. However, you will have to consider how this singular focus might impact your ability to change careers in the future. Research is your friend before you make this choice, as the thesis you produce will follow you for years.

Chapter 6

Which One?

Research, Research, RESEARCH! Know your university, know your field, and most importantly: **know yourself**.

Something to consider in this regard is your personality and work preferences. Do you enjoy working with others? Do you prefer being alone and conducting independent research? What is it that you hope to get out of the experience? What are your career prospects? Having the answers to these questions will help you identify which option is best for you.

There are a few rules that you should follow in terms of preparing for each possible graduation avenue. When it comes to testing, working with and speaking to your peers as often as possible is advisable. Read as much as you can, but be selective with what you read. Refrain from inundating your brain with information that will not work to your advantage during assessments. Knowledge is virtually infinite. It is impossible for you to know everything on every topic in your field of study. Follow the recommended reading list and build on it if you can. Create a few mock essay plans so that you have several outlines in mind when it is time for your assessment.

Writing a master's thesis or publishable paper is the course of action you will take with a thesis-based or research-based program. Similar to a dissertation in terms of how you research something original, your thesis requires efficient planning. Once you have chosen your thesis question and conducted preliminary research, you must start compiling your sources. Review the current literature relevant to your thesis and select primary and secondary sources. Ensure you understand the thesis requirements, and then start crafting an outline. When you have a solid outline, you can work on your timeline. Be honest with yourself about how much writing you can achieve in a day. For some, writing just a few hundred words daily is better than writing thousands of words every couple of days in spurts. If you focus on making small incremental progress each day, the progression of writing will be natural. You will not struggle to remember what you covered, and you will not get tied down with the minutiae. Give yourself enough time to review your work compared to the thesis requirements your university has for graduation, while paying particular attention to your opening statements and your conclusion as they are judged the most.

For both options, remember your SMART goals. Craft a plan to prepare for exams or research before you start graduate school. You should show up day one with a general idea of which you will do, how you will do it, and the timeline you intend to do it in. Print it off and frame the plan if you need to.

Forming a Graduate Committee

A graduate committee, also known as a special committee, is responsible for directing your studies as well as overseeing your thesis or comprehensive exams. This committee comprises a chair or primary advisor, committee members,

Chapter 6

and ad hoc committee members. Forming your committee is entirely your responsibility, and there are protocols that you need to adhere to. As with everything covered up until this point, this will vary per the policies of your university and your field of study. However, there are some general guidelines for selecting your graduate committee members.

Most universities want you to declare who your chair will be within the first month of starting your program. Since they are primary on your progress, they are responsible for ensuring you are prepared for either graduate route. Your chair needs to be a faculty member. They can be a current faculty or, in some cases, a retired emeritus professor. They should be an expert in your field, and they will represent you to the rest of the department when you need funding, lab space, or if you need someone to talk to.

You usually have until the end of your second semester to select the rest of your committee. The additional members represent the minor portion of your degree. Whether it is for testing or thesis, the additional members should have varied expertise to ensure you have complete mastery of the field. You can also select faculty members from another institution to serve as ad hoc members of your committee. However, you typically want to limit your overall committee to three.

Selecting your committee is one of the most important decisions you will make regarding your graduate studies, so do not feel obligated to select all your committee members immediately. Consider your options well, and consult your graduate program coordinator for advice until you finalize your selection. Be aware that this committee will be responsible for guiding as well as assessing your progress. Depending on the type of program you pick, they will be responsible for everything from directing your coursework to conducting assessments and the review of your thesis. Avoid people whom your gut feeling tells you they do not have your best interest at heart, as too often People of Color are mistreated by senior academics. Furthermore, their reputations could hurt or bolster your career for years after you graduate, so research them, get to know them, and decide who is best for you and your vision of the future.

Utilizing your committee and working closely with each member is crucial for success. Your chair will be your primary academic advisor, and you should work toward establishing a solid relationship with them. They will be a sounding board for your thoughts and theories as well as a mentor for your research. You should also turn to them for advice regarding your thesis. Ensure that you select faculty members who know the processes involved and have the time to take up the roles and responsibilities in their positions. You can always substitute a committee member if they are otherwise indisposed, but this detracts from the compounding value you gain from developing discussions with these members. It is also not the easiest procedure to get clearance for, particularly if you must replace a committee member who disagrees.

Chapter 6

Their opinion, however, should not stop you from changing a committee member if you feel that this would be best for you. This journey is about **your** future, and you cannot be more concerned about stepping on other people's toes more than your future success. Too often, people who do not fit into the typical white male, heterosexual, protestant archetype feel they need to limit their voice around others so nobody labels them the malcontent. We think if we step out of line then they will push us back into a box, but that is the thinking of a bygone age. The need to keep things serene at all times, often at the expense of your feelings, is part of years of preconditioning from society. However, you donned the fuck'em armor, and you will not allow people to dictate your life. Do not be afraid to rock the boat. Be polite and respectful at all times, but advocate for yourself **fiercely**. If things get really bad, then it may be time for a change. Speak with your chair about the issue and voice your concerns regarding the member you want to change. Go to the dean if need be and file a complaint. Afterward, you will need to find a new committee member to take their place and fill out forms detailing the request's reason. It will then be up to your Graduate Program Director or Academic Coordinator to approve the change or suggest a route for conflict management.

There can be times where the problem is your chair, so the avenue towards resolution is even harder. Storytime: During my doctoral studies, my original primary advisor and I disagreed more than once about how prepared I was and what steps I needed to complete to move forward. At one point, they wanted me to take another year or two of classes for no justifiable reason to me or the department chair. As I continued to advocate for myself, they became quite upset, and told us both they refused to work with me any further. The department chair expected me to be upset, but they did not know I prepared for multiple contingencies. I already had three names ready to replace my advisor, and I had two new ones within days.

I tell you that story because I want you to learn a few lessons. First, advocate for yourself because you are the only person in the room who will. Second, not everyone will appreciate a Student of Color who stands up for themselves. Third, you need to be prepared for how others will react to you. Fourth, if you plan properly then others cannot stand in your path. Fifth, **never take off your armor.**

Not all conflict is bad, and not everything has to escalate into hurt feelings or bruised egos. Maintain your professionalism and do what is best for you. In my situation, I hold no ill will toward my previous advisor and have remained respectful toward them in all subsequent interactions. If you experience a similar problem, and a resolution is afforded to you and the committee member in question, consider taking it. However, stick to your choice if you feel the working relationship is unsalvageable or a bad fit. It could hamper the progress of your thesis or mastery of the coursework. Never forget that this is your journey, not theirs.

Chapter 6

Writing Your Thesis

It can be daunting when a professor sits you down, looks you in the eyes, and says your thesis needs to be one-hundred pages or more of original research that advances the field. I still remember when my first master's advisor told me that and the nonchalant way he said it. I remember thinking it would take years to research and write, but I realized it was doable once I started to put in the work.

Writing a master's thesis is different than any other form of writing you have done in your life, even if you completed honor's classes as I did during my undergraduate study. Furthermore, I cannot fully prepare you for everything your thesis will throw at you since every field is different. However, I do have some tips to assist my friends no matter their major:

- ♦ Know what you want to research, write early, and then start working on it as soon as possible.
- ♦ Talk to experts in your field to ensure your research is novel, and check in with them as you progress (you might even grow your support network while doing so).
- ♦ Communicate with your graduate committee constantly; if things change they should know first.
- ♦ Depending on your field, research three days a week and write the other three. Do **not** disturb the sanctity of your rest day.

- If your major is research heavy, then frontload as much as you can then move on to writing.
- Use chunking while writing: thirty minutes of writing and ten minutes of rest.
- Lean on your support network when things get rough, and yes, they will get rough.

There are countless additional tips that other academics in your field can offer, and I encourage you to reach out to them. If you have an advisor doing their job, they should properly advise you on the best course of action to complete your thesis correctly. It is to their benefit that you do well because it makes them and the department look good, so you can trust their advice.

If you follow all of these tips—including program-specific steps your advisor gives you—then you will find writing your master's thesis is doable as I did. Once you are finished writing your thesis, you will want to take time to edit and revise it, because you will have to submit the thesis to your graduate committee. They will read every page and judge you on your research and writing before setting a date for you to defend your thesis.

The term defense is a misnomer, as you are really celebrating your accomplishment at this point. If your committee examined your thesis and set a defense date then they already agreed you demonstrated a mastery, and at this point they just need you to prove what they already suspect. So go into the defense with the mindset they are celebrating how awesome you are, because that is what a defense is. That said, a defense can last hours, and some questions can be quite probing. However, they are attempting to find the limits of your knowledge more so than prove you are inadequate. If you selected an appropriate committee then it will be filled with tenured professors with decades of experience, so naturally, they will know more than you at this point in your career. You are not an imposter if you do not know as much as them during your defense; what is essential is that you know everything in your thesis and on your topic.

After completing your thesis defense, some programs may want you to publish the entire thesis or publish a paper or two based on your research, and if so, then you have one last hurdle to jump over before you graduate.

Is Publication Important?

Publications are important to academics in nearly all fields when it comes to graduate school. While publication is not a requirement for the completion of graduate studies across the US, some institutions require graduate students to publish their thesis or a paper before graduating. If you plan to study abroad, make sure you know all of the conferral requirements before applying. For the US, most universities require an upload to ProQuest or some other online repository that pseudo-publishes your work for other academics to access. Remember, your thesis advances your field, and it cannot do that if you and your committee members are the only people who know about it.

Nonetheless, publication is still vital to your future success as a researcher. For many, the thought of having their name on a published paper is enough encouragement. You would not have had the drive to come this far if you did not desire to acquire that stamp of authority in your field. Publishing papers is the best way to establish yourself as an expert in your field, and your publications can open doors for future career advancements. Suppose you have a goal to develop a career in research or academia. In that case, publications tell potential employers to view you as a strong contender compared to others with the same degree but no publications. A publication demonstrates you researched a vast amount of sources on your subject, and you fully understood all of them while you did it. That in-depth knowledge reflects your mastery of the field. Additionally, publications benefit you if you decide to pursue your doctorate later. Having publications in peer-reviewed journals is a good indicator of your ability to handle the research required for a dissertation. It also shows that you are invested in the field. It showcases your grit and determination, making you a great candidate. The relevant admissions officers will know just how hard you worked to have your paper published, especially if you publish this work in a credible journal.

There are additional benefits to publishing your work as a paper or series of papers. Chief among them, you demonstrate to others like you that it is possible. A year after publishing my first paper, I had a high school student contact me about getting a copy since she could not afford to pay for it, but she wanted the research for something she was working on. I gladly gave her a copy. After corresponding with her, I found out she had plans to one day become a researcher, and I hope our conversation inspired her to pursue her dreams. Like her, others may need your work to complete their research or it could help someone on their path. Plus, if your research is well done, you will be referenced in books and other journals, thus spreading your name across the academic world even further, which will help your future career prospects.

There is the added benefit of growing your professional network. Most STEM research is collaborative, and you might work with a co-author or a team of them. Together you will complete the study and paper. The effort could lead toward forming strong bonds with one another during the research process. Even papers written with one author can help as you might present those papers at conferences, and you will meet others with similar interest. I have met some wonderful intellectuals at dozens of conferences over the years, and seeing them again at another conference is always something I look forward to. Some even helped in additional publications or papers as well. Like me, you will meet others who look like you or who have lived similar life experiences who will be more than willing to help a new researcher in their field.

Your New Journey

Expanding your peer network is essential for future endeavors, making this crucial for long-term goals.

Do not allow the process of manuscript submission deter you from taking this step in your academic career. There are numerous guides on the process, and read up on the process if your advisor does not help you. Always proofread your work, you can even use an AI to help, then send it off to a peer or two for feedback. You want at least one other person to read your work and give you honest feedback, no fluff as that will not help you. Make the necessary revisions and then identify journals willing to publish your niche. Read a few articles in that journal to make sure your paper is appropriate. Read and understand the submission requirements as well, as many editors will desk reject if the submission is wrong. After familiarizing yourself with the journal you can submit your manuscript.

One of two things will happen after you submit the manuscript. You either will not hear from the editor for quite some time while they review it or they will get back to you with their comments immediately and reject the paper. Graduates often feel deflated when they receive feedback regarding their manuscript and you should try to avoid this downward mental spiral. Feedback is a good thing, even if their choice of words is negative. Most academics think they are offering constructive criticism, and their words are meant to demonstrate they seriously considered your manuscript. The typical response is R&R: revise and resubmit. The reviewers

Chapter 6

for your paper will have comments on structure or wording throughout, and they will ask you to resubmit the paper. That just means they want you to perfect it before publishing it, but there are cases where a reviewer is just trying to force you to mirror their style or research. Read through the comments carefully, contact the editor if you suspect impropriety, and if they attempt to force you then simply withdraw the paper and submit it elsewhere. This is still your journey, and you will not let others dictate your path or research. If everything is done properly then the revisions should improve your paper, and once they are complete the journal will happily publish your paper. Once they do, be sure to let me know. I would love to hear about it!

If journal publication seems too problematic, you can test your writing and research through conference presentations. Conferences are a fantastic way to connect to others in your field, because academic societies usually organize them with a focus on one subject. Thus, you will meet others from around the world who exclusively love your subject as much as you do. I traveled the world giving lectures and presenting papers, and each time I met remarkable scholars who expanded my thinking. Furthermore, you can use a paper presentation to test your research with a small group of scholars who will offer critiques. Some of their criticism will be helpful, some will not, but overall, you will get a sense of how your field will receive your research. Thus, you can make adjustments based on the discussion afterward.

Some larger conferences also offer posters for junior scholars, and some world-changing research began as a poster, blossomed into a presentation paper, and the study was eventually published in top-tier journals. Other smaller publications include blog posts, podcasts, newsletters, and even social media posts. All of these can decimate your research and increase your network for your life's journey.

No matter your career goals, publication is important because it enhances your field and yourself. Look for avenues of publication during graduate school, and they will pay dividends years down the line.

Graduate Certificates

While working on your master's degree, or possibly a terminal choice, you can also earn a graduate certificate. A graduate certificate is different from a degree because it is a certification that proves you have one particular skill. For example, you could earn a project management certificate after twelve credits while pursuing your MBA. Typically, the only prerequisite is that you have a bachelor's degree, and it does not have to be in a related field if the certification is terminal. Contrary to a degree, there is no thesis requirement, and any tests are limited in scope to the certificate.

Most certifications are fifteen credits or less, and they are great for working professionals who want to attend a few classes, get certified, and pursue a promotion or career move.

Chapter 6

They foster critical thinking, reading, and writing in students, and those who earn them prove to potential employers they have clear oral and written communication skills. The classes usually meet at night, can be taken part-time, and are tailored to a specific job. The brevity of certification means the cost is a lot less than a full degree, and they are an excellent alternative to the traditional degree route for students who know exactly what they want to do after graduation.

Nearly all professions have a certification of some kind, but not all universities offer them. It will take searching what the university offers to see if a certificate is possible in addition to or in lieu of a master's degree. Furthermore, it may be possible to create your own certification at certain liberal arts colleges that allow for innovative degrees.

It is possible to pursue a certificate while considering if graduate school is the right thing for you. The classrooms and instruction are the same, and you only need to attend all required courses. The credits taken for the certificate are transferable to a degree, and that means you can take the first twelve credits, see if that university or program is the right fit for you, and continue with a degree or leave, depending on your experience. Consider if this option is best for you early, and plan accordingly as it could set you on a future career path or help you avoid a critical error.

Peer Support

I want you to lean on your support system throughout the entire master's degree process. Chief among them needs to be your peers. While earning your master's is not as difficult as many think it is, it is still hard work. It is a rigorous process requiring your utmost attention to make the most out of it. Leaning on your support system—especially other students—will keep things in perspective. It is easy to think that you are the only one climbing the mountain when everyone else is on the other side. However, that is what isolation does to you. It puts this gargantuan mountain between you and the people that have the potential to help you climb. When you engage with your peers and seek their advice, they become vital role players in your ascent. If you cannot rely on the peers in your department then lean on others elsewhere from other universities or even other countries. I guarantee that if you look hard enough, you will find at least two peers somewhere in the world you can rely on during your journey to greatness.

You can tell from my writing that I am a positive person, and that is not because only good things happened to me. Instead, it took practice and relying on others. I write that because I want you to work on and keep a positive mental outlook on the future. When you engage with your peers, ensure they have a similar perspective so you can help each other maintain positivity. That does not mean you need to put on a brave face just to fit in or appease everyone, and you both should be able to voice your frustrations at momentary obstacles. However, if you or they are the person continuously focusing on the negative, then you will only bring each other down. Before you know it, both of you are contemplating leaving school or changing careers simply because things are hard. When you feel like those around you can no longer support you, it is time to start offering them support. Ask yourself whether or not you have been taking more than you gave, because you do not want to be that person either. Sometimes, the best gifts are the gifts we give to others. Sharing your time and lending an ear to someone while you are in the midst of your strife will allow you to problem-solve together. If you both look at it as working the problem as a team, then you can find a solution to all your problems that does not involve abandoning your journey.

If you maintain a curious, problem-solving mindset, you can devise solutions to what stresses you out or sets you back. Keep your energy vibrant and positive while you succeed as a master's student.

*

Overall, the journey to completing a master's or certificate program is a lot easier than most people think. Becoming accustomed to doing as much research as possible and making informed decisions will help you find a great university and program. Furthermore, that skill will serve you throughout your academic career as you elevate yourself to a level where this will be expected. Forming your committee will be one of the more critical aspects. The faculty members

Your New Journey

on this committee will supervise and approve your thesis, so your selection is crucial. Form a positive peer group, and lean on them throughout the process. Having people to turn to or lean on during your journey is essential for your future success.

EARNING YOUR DOCTORATE

Doctor. It has a nice ring to it. The only "D" word I prefer more is Dad. However, getting a doctorate is about more than a title; it is the apex of academia and cements you as an expert in your field. It demonstrates your passion, your ability, and your work ethic. Some, like me, pursue a doctorate after completing their master's. Others planned from the beginning to get one after undergraduate. Whatever your path, if you have decided to pursue this, then I will give you some tools to help along on this journey.

A PhD is a research-intensive doctorate. There are also applied doctorates with less research and writing that focus more on what that job entails. However, this book will focus on the PhD, but many of the suggestions are applicable to all doctorates. Quick overview, a PhD typically requires 72 credits or more. 45-60 of these are earned in the classroom, while the remaining credits are earned through research and completing your dissertation. You take comprehensive exams, similar to the master's test-out option, once you complete your coursework. Afterward, you submit a prospectus that outlines your proposed research before writing your dissertation. Depending on the field, a dissertation could be a hundred pages or close to a thousand. Research your university, and know every requirement and when it is expected before you step foot on that campus.

Before we start, consider if you are making the right choice. Not everyone needs a PhD, and in most professions, it makes you overqualified. Consider your career goals carefully before beginning this journey. If so, then I will talk about forming a PhD committee, comps, writing a prospectus, researching your dissertation, and preparing for graduation.

Making the Right Choice

If you have read this far then you already have most of the tips down, and you will have planned before beginning a doctoral program. However, many complete their master's and get excited about having just completed their studies. They realize there is so much more to learn and get excited about the next step. For some, that could entail a step away from academia to begin or continue their career. For others, it could mean pursuing a PhD. Personally, I did both and it worked out pretty great, but you have to decide which is best for you.

People often ask whether or not they should take a break between their various certifications, and there is no right or wrong answer. As with anything in your life, your decision will come down to your circumstances and goals. If you have the stamina to keep going, and the resources to do so, go ahead. When I write of resources, this has more to do with whether or not you need to get back to providing part or all of the income for your family. That, of course, is if you have a family dependent on you. Regarding the resources, or funding, that you will need to complete your PhD, you should seek this from your university. Alternatively, you can approach any organization that falls into the categories discussed in Chapter 2.

With that in mind, and to answer the question, it all depends on your goals, circumstances, and preferences. If you feel as though taking a break in between your master's and your PhD will give you the time to decompress and get recalibrated with the so-called "regular world," then go ahead and do that. If you feel that this time away could potentially halt your momentum and prevent you from achieving your long-term academic goals, then you should consider enrolling in a PhD program fairly soon after graduating with your master's. Some universities offer automatic enrollment or initially register you as a master's student while you are working on your doctorate. Either way, review your goals at this point. Sit down and think about what you want to achieve and whether or not earning your PhD contributes to them. Also, consider whether your goals have changed since you graduated with your master's. Your mind will have been trained to review the facts and to be flexible. You will have more of an ability to change your mind in accordance with new facts than ever before. This means that the information, people, and circumstances, which you will have been exposed to during your master's program, may have changed your overall view of the world and your career. There is nothing wrong with stepping back once you have your bachelor's or master's in hand and saying, "that is enough."

I want you to ask yourself: Do I need a doctorate? I want you to ask this early because this is the hardest of all academic journeys, and countless people begin this path only to fall off when they discover it is too difficult, and think to themselves later: "I do not need this headache, so I quit." That label of quitter will follow you internally and haunt you when you sleep. I want you to thrive, not lose sleep over something you could have avoided. Review your academic and career goals carefully, and make sure this is what you want. If so, then I want you to remind yourself throughout this journey that you choose this for your future happiness.

What is a PhD Committee?

A PhD committee is similar to a master's committee. If you skipped the previous chapter, you will find a wealth of information on the matter by reading Chapter 6. That being said, you probably already understand the committee structure if you earned your master's. On this level your committee will be made of five, sometimes more, professors who will work together to ensure you learn everything you need to one day add that prefix to your name.

As with a master's committee, you will nominate your chair within the first semester or so of beginning your PhD program. This person will be responsible for guiding your academic career and should have the time to act as chair of your committee. Their responsibilities will include:

- Advising you regarding your prospectus and helping you navigate the approval process.
- Guiding the preparation, submission, and defense of your dissertation.
- Having the necessary experience in, and knowledge of, the dissertation policies.
- Helping you select the other committee members.
- Tracking your progress each semester as successful (SP) or unsuccessful (NP).
- Guiding your ethical principles throughout your research.
- Assisting you with your data collection and the analysis thereof.
- Leading your lab and overseeing your publications.

There is much more your primary advisor will need to do, but these are the core areas that you should ensure they are willing to cover during their time as your committee chair. When it comes to research proposal structuring and formatting, your chair will act as your sole advisor on the subject. Communicating with your advisor as often as possible is essential. You will be working hand in hand for the duration of your program, and you should pay close attention to their advice regarding the process.

Consider your chair as the middle ground between you and the rest of your committee members. They will alert the rest of the committee when there is writing they need to review and if there are any upcoming committee meetings to attend. This faculty member will be invaluable, especially during the four phases of a doctorate. These periods include:

- 45-60 course credits.
- Prospectus drafting, submission, and defense.
- Researching and writing your manuscript.
- Defense of your final dissertation.

Typically, you have until the end of your third semester to select the remaining committee members. As mentioned in the previous chapter, it is important to take your time and consider who would be best for the roles in question. Your chair will advise you in this regard, but the decision should yours. You may be able to select your committee with minimal interference. However, you might have to choose your committee from a list of pre-approved members. Again, this will depend on your university and program.

Strike a balance between taking your time to find the best committee members and taking too long to do so. You want to be certain of their suitability, but you do not want to prolong the matter and waste valuable time. Remember, you can always submit a request to change a committee member if, for some reason, they are unable to fulfill their duties or your personalities do not agree with one another. Your first option for recourse will always be conflict management, but if this is not suited to the situation at hand, you will need to make the call to have a member replaced. Just bear in mind that you will have to find a new member before submitting your request for member replacement. Think of this as a business decision; if the committee member cannot help you then cut them for someone else. They are tenured professors anyway, so they should not take it too personally if you replace them with someone more suitable.

A critical factor in selecting your committee members is their roles concerning your comprehensive exams. Comps, as they are often called, are a series of exams similar to the ones master's students take for graduation, and most departments award a master's degree after you complete them. Your committee members will act as the testers for your exams, and they will want to ensure you know every facet of your subject. Thus, you will want to make sure they know it as well. Selecting the proper committee ensures they prepare you for the exams, and if they do their job, you will succeed. If you fail, that means **they failed you.**

With the right committee in hand, you are prepared to attend the required classes for your PhD and study for your compressive exams.

Comprehensive Exams: What to Know

Comps are general assessments that take place over a few days. They are there to test how well you have mastered a specific field of study. Comps can be written, oral, or both. Most graduate programs will give you at least a year to prepare for comps, and they are not for a grade. You either pass or fail. Put simply, you mastered the material or you did not.

Now, there are a few key distinctions between comps for a master's and a doctorate. While master's students will have comps that lead to the conferral of their certification, doctorates look at comps as a stepping stone. Students working toward their PhD will have to pass comps before moving on to the dissertation. Both have similar setups: major and minor fields. Your advisor should oversee your major, and your committee members will test your minor. Together, they will decide if you pass. Work with them to determine what classes you should take while you prepare for comps, maybe even take their classes if it is their expertise, and together you can form the structure of your exams. If you do too poorly on comps but barely pass, some universities may pass you with a master's but decline to let you continue. Offering the degree as a consolation prize, while crediting the department with another graduate as they remove you. However, you will avoid that outcome by preparing for the tests properly.

How you get ready for these exams will vary depending on your field, but the most important thing is that you begin preparing for these exams as early as possible. Do not put it off, thinking that you can catch up later. Start reading as your committee gives you the information regarding your comps. They will usually provide multiple reading lists to help you prepare for your comps. They should provide you with relevant texts and specific topics that you will do as much research and reading on as possible. Your advisor will expect you to find more documents and books worth reading for your exams. Read it all, take notes, and use that year to prepare as much as possible.

Nailing Your Comps

There are multiple exams that you might be expected to take as a PhD student. Some doctoral programs, such as those in the engineering field, may require you to complete a Qualifying Exam before entering the program. For programs that do not require this before commencement, you will likely have a comprehensive exam that aims to assess your expertise in your program's theory and the relevant methodology. Your special committee will determine the content of this exam and recommend reading lists for you to review before the exam. Your chair will be responsible for coordinating these efforts, and this is why it is imperative that you pick someone knowledgeable in your field of study. No matter the amount or type, there are general steps you can take to pass them.

You will have a recommended amount of time to study for this exam, but you will have to schedule the oral portion by completing a form declaring your intention. The exam structure is different across the US, more so across the world. In most cases, comps are split into two portions: written and oral. For the written half, you can expect two to four questions covering the material you should be well versed in from coursework. Furthermore, you will be allotted a certain amount of time to complete one of the following:

- Literature review
- Grant proposal
- Journal article (Publishable)
- Multimedia project
- Dissertation proposal
- Theoretical paper
- Methodological exposition
- Answer probing question about your field
- Policy paper

Knowing your institution's policies and what they expect from PhD students is vital to success. There may be additional options not expressed in the list above, so look into it thoroughly. Nonetheless, you will be required to write responses to the questions mentioned just before the above list, and you will need to use one of the listed formats. These responses are typically no more than 70 pages in total.

Take time to read the recommended material and discuss everything with your peers who are working toward similar targets. You should also meet with your chair to address any concerns regarding the upcoming assessment. Once your committee hands you the exam questions, you may have about two weeks or more to answer each question. They expect you will circulate your answers once finished. After you answers all questions satisfactorily, you will move on to your oral exam.

Chapter 7

> **SIDE NOTE:** You will be required to set a date for your oral exam before any of the examinations begin. Give yourself enough time to work on the written portion of the exam because all questions should, ideally, be completed two weeks prior to your oral exam.

Many People of Color worry regarding the oral portion, as we have our own way of talking. One professor once commented, "I do not speak like a graduate student." I had to let them know: "I will always speak like myself." I suggest you have a similar outlook, and avoid falling into the code switching trope. However, if you focus on building a good relationship with your committee, you will come to understand their manner of speaking and engaging with you and vice versa. Comprehension is everything where your comps are concerned. Having a clear picture of what will be expected of you and keeping in close contact with your committee will ensure you pass. Remember, not only is your committee responsible for setting the exam, but they are also responsible for determining whether you have proven your mastery of the material. If you fail your comps, you will have to wait 3 months to retake them. This process may vary for your university, but this is the consensus. Once again, research your university and understand all the steps.

If you opted for a hybrid or virtual program that allows you to undergo part of your PhD remotely, you could request that you take comps through video conferencing platforms. However, this is not an exam that you can cheat on. Trust they will be able to tell whether you accomplished what you set out to do. They are experts so no bullshitting. Weigh the pros and cons of this setup. Whether you are comfortable with this arrangement or not will play a role in how you cope with your exams. Even if you are undergoing the bulk of your PhD remotely, keep those lines of communication open with your committee, and do not wait for them to contact you.

Comps are not strictly pass/fail at some universities. You can pass, conditionally pass, conditionally fail, or unanimously fail. If you pass, well, you pass. Well done! If you receive a conditional pass, your committee will provide a few conditions you need to meet before they declare an official pass. If you conditionally fail, your committee will often approve you to retake the exam in about three months after correcting whatever condition caused you to fail. However, if you have what is known as a unanimous failure, your studies can come to a complete halt. You will have to petition the dean or department head to continue studying at the university. Failure like this is incredibly rare and only occurs when there is a complete lack of progress or advancement of knowledge in your field. If this happens, you made no effort, and your advisor failed to acknowledge that when they scheduled your exams which means they failed in their duties as well.

However, failure is **not** an option for one of my friends! Read every book they give you and create notes for each. I want you to use the following structure in your notes:

- Overall argument of the book or paper.
- Chapter breakdown with a quick summary of each.
- Argument of each chapter.
- Sources used throughout.
- Connection to other works.
- How it contributes to the field.
- If you agree/disagree with this work and why.
- How do other experts view this work?

Each diamond point should have a detailed paragraph or multiple as needed. Ask your advisor if your field needs additional notes on specific things, such as lab-specific measurements or data you need to quantify. Once done, you will find that some books will have multiple pages of notes, and that is perfect. Here is why, you will start preparing for these exams a year, sometimes two, before you take the exam. That means you will forget a lot of what you read early on. Unless you plan to read and reread an entire book, then this method gives you the layout to read them once, take notes, and reread your notes the final weeks before your exam. I preferred reading five pages of notes over three hundred when I prepped for my exams. Furthermore, when you are working on your dissertation, there will be a section for a literature review, and the notes you are taking now can be the foundation for your review versus you having to reread the books. Thus, this method ensures you are fully prepared for your PhD's short and long-term portions.

I told you I look out for my friends.

Your New Journey

After creating your detailed notes, you will print them off and put them all in one binder. Read it from cover to cover until you almost memorize everything inside. When prepping for comps, I want you to reach out to your peer network. Bounce ideas for questions off of one another, and then have them judge you based on your answers. After sitting in classrooms listening to professors for years, you all know what it sounds like if someone is confidently answering a question or if they have no idea what they are talking about. Furthermore, your peers should know the correct answer if they are in your department or field. If you are struggling to answer a question, review your notes; if your notes are the problem then redo them to see what you missed. Keep this process up for about six to three months before your scheduled exams.

One month before comps, you should sit down with your chair and ask them to give you a mock exam. Plan for two to three hours, and have them ask you as many probing questions as possible. Take their criticism in stride, as they want you to pass as much as you do. If you pass, great. Keep studying. If you fail, that is great too. You identified your weak spot a month early, so you have time to fix it before the exam. Study, Study, **STUDY**.

If you follow all of these steps, you will pass the academic hazing known as comprehensive exams and be ready for the next phase of your journey.

Chapter 7

Crafting Your Prospectus

Your dissertation prospectus is a document you submit to your committee that details your plan for completing your PhD. The prospectus describes what you plan to research, how you intend to conduct it, what you will write for your dissertation, and the timeline for completing everything. It is not a contract, however, as it is only your preliminary idea of what you plan to do. Plans change and everyone knows that, so if your final dissertation is different, that is fine. The prospectus proves to the university that you have a plan to get this done. While some want a draft within the first year, the majority want it after you pass your comprehensive exams as they now know you have a mastery of the field. Every university has requirements for how and when they want the prospectus, and you should incorporate the completion of the prospectus into your plan before you begin the program.

Before you submit your prospectus to your committee, you should meet with everyone to brainstorm your ideas. It is important to have a clearer understanding of the dissertation process for your department. Having all of the information and the confidence boost provided to you by your committee is well worth the minimal delay by calling this meeting. However, you should have a general mind map of your dissertation's subject matter before applying to the university. So look at this meeting as your opportunity to finally spill all the ideas in your head to everyone involved and clarify what you want to do. At best, your committee should tweak your ideas to be novel and innovative, but if they want you to revamp your plan for their vanity projects then reconsider having them on your committee. If the new idea can genuinely help in your career and academic goals, consider it, but if not, then stick to your guns and respectfully remind them this is your journey, not theirs. However, most professors already know this, and they will be supportive of whatever ideas you have with minor changes intended to help you in ways that only their years of expertise can see. You can get to work on your prospectus after your meeting.

Begin with your title and consider it carefully. Does it encapsulate everything that you will cover in your dissertation? Is it easy to understand? Is it precise and concise? Make sure it alludes to the central question of your dissertation. Next, think carefully about your thesis question, as it is the foundation of everything. You do not necessarily have to pose a question here. You can write a paragraph-long statement that explains the research your dissertation will address. Ensure the title and question work in unison. If your committee reviews your dissertation and finds that the content of your paper has little to do with the title and subsequent central question, you are going to have a hard time defending your prospectus and getting final approval. More is not always better here. If you can get the message across in fewer words, do that. Keep it **succinct** and **accurate**.

Your next section should speak to the current literature in your field and how your dissertation will tackle methodological, critical, and theoretical concerns. Simply put, this is where you convince the reader that your research project is needed to advance the understanding of the subject matter. Remember those notes I wanted you to write for comps? You can use those to form the bulk, if not all, of your literature review for the relevant works. The point of the review, however, is not just to show how much you have read but how much has not been researched on your topic. Even if there was a lot, your review could show a dozen researchers looked at this one way, but they all ignored the approach you plan to take.

The following section entails your proposed methodological processes and the feasibility of your project. Your committee wants to know how you plan to conduct your research and whether the methods you plan to use are viable. Give as much detail as possible here, as they will significantly judge this section. If you have yet to learn how you will conduct your research or where the relevant primary sources are, then you are proving you are unprepared to continue. Take your time and consider this part of the plan well, and ask your committee members what they suggest instead of writing anything and being wrong.

A potential section—and one that students often fail to see the importance of—is the "why" behind your dissertation. Why is your research so important? What will happen to the field because of it? How will your research project help you explore further projects in the future? How will it help advance your career prospects as an academic or otherwise? Demonstrating your investment in the subject matter can have a profoundly positive impact, and prove how serious you are about completing the dissertation. This section will be followed by an exploration of your primary and secondary sources as well as any other literature that might not be directly linked to your subject but will assist in formulating your methodologies.

These are some of the most common sections, but your university or field may require more. When you meet with your committee, they should tell you what to expect from them and what they expect from you. Furthermore, ask for a copy of a successful prospectus from each. That will give you a general idea of what they expect yours to look like, and you can plan accordingly.

> **SIDE NOTE:** Your committee will advise you on the proper way to prepare a prospectus in accordance with the university's best practices. They will also indicate an appropriate length and how they want you to defend it.

After completing your prospectus, you will have to defend it. Similar to the master's thesis, the term defense is a misnomer that really should get a new name. Instead, this is a discussion where your committee confirms you have a detailed plan to research and complete your dissertation. Very few fail a prospectus defense, and the few who did either gave up or their professors failed to prepare them, usually some combination of both. If you follow the steps in this section, then you will have the minimum required to pass a prospectus defense and move on with writing your dissertation.

From Research to Dissertation

It is time! The culmination of most doctorates is completing a dissertation, a book-length manuscript filled with original research and writing. Some universities, especially outside of the US, require the completion of multiple papers published in top-tier journals, however. Make sure you know what your program requires before you begin. No matter what, a PhD is about imaginative research. Even medical practitioners who want to put the acronym after their name must complete a fair amount of research. This process will take the bulk of your journey, and will require sleepless nights and days when you question why you had this idea. However, if you followed my advice and made sure this was something you really wanted to do, and a topic you were truly passionate about, then you will have the motivation to see this journey through until the end.

The process is relatively straightforward: you will spend years researching your dissertation topic; your research will focus on answering the thesis question you developed that will revolutionize your field; once you and your advisor agree you have done enough research to answer that question, you will begin writing; some universities allow you to continue research while you are in the writing phase; finish writing the dissertation; edit and revise; submit to your committee; defend and graduate. It seems so easy that I can put it all in one, albeit long, sentence.

Sorry, but as I said in the beginning, this is the longest and hardest journey for all academics to walk. However, there are some ways to ensure you thrive while completing it.

Starting with the research, you should have created a plan long before you started the program; however, some of you may have purchased this book after you started or you do not like to plan too early. Even after reading my book, some readers undoubtedly will finish comps and finally ask themselves, what will I research? Luckily, if you completed all of those readings then you should have formulated an idea of the field and the gaps within the research of others. When you write the prospectus, you should detail those gaps, which is your first avenue to begin research. While it is great to lean on your committee as needed, this is the solo portion of the journey. They will expect you to know what you want to research. Some may have vanity projects they wish to work on themselves, but do you want to walk someone else's path? Take the initiative and go out on a limb with your research. Let it take you down a rabbit hole, and enjoy the process as you do. There are times a research idea becomes a tangent into unrelated territory, and you might formulate personal side projects to work on after you complete your dissertation. Save those ideas and what you find elsewhere, and continue with your primary research.

Chapter 7

Research, tangents, more research, it is all part of what it means to earn a doctorate. Do not allow it to distract you from the material you are supposed to cover, but give in to curiosity when it comes up. You are an aspiring academic after all, so enjoy the fun of learning as much as possible. That is how you keep the passion for your field alive. Additionally, when it comes time to defend your dissertation, you will have aside information to discuss not in your manuscript that shows how much more you know on the subject. It all demonstrates your mastery of—and interest in—the field.

The research, even the side projects, are crucial when it is time to write your dissertation. As you prepared for comps you read dozens—sometimes hundreds—of books and articles on your field. All those readings exposed you to what academic writing looks like, the jargon your specialty requires, and the criticism experts had for the works of others. Look over the notes I suggested you write if you need a refresher, and use the mistakes and successes of others to structure your dissertation.

I want you to assess your typing speed. While you might have an average typing speed for social media or writing personal thoughts, you have never completed dissertation writing. Thus, take a day or two and assess how long it takes to write a page. You might find it can take hours to complete a single page, a week for a table. The increase in time is because you are carefully considering your sources and wording as you write. Once you know your average typing speed, you can plan accordingly for how long it will take to write a chapter or the whole thing. Speed will come later, so allow your writing to evolve naturally. Do not get bogged down too much with the wording of everything as this is only the first draft.

The burn draft. Even if it takes a year to write, the first draft of your dissertation is for your eyes only. Do not send it to anyone, even your best friend. Literally burn it if you need to. If you are writing chapter by chapter or the whole dissertation at once, the first draft is meant to get all the thoughts and research out of your head and onto paper; however, the first draft will be incoherent and have a lot of word vomit. Save a copy of the first draft, open a new document, use split screen, and begin working on the second draft. **DO NOT COPY-PASTE!** Write your second draft into the new document as you read the first, and I guarantee you will see sections that make no sense, need to be rewritten, or removed outright. Do not worry as much about time. Writing a chapter after you already completed it will only take a few days, so the second draft is a lot faster to write than the first. After completing the second draft of your dissertation you can finally send it to others for their comments and suggestions.

Give yourself sufficient time to edit your dissertation before submitting it to your committee. Restructuring your chapters might take more precedence than it did while you were writing the first draft, but it can save your entire manuscript. If you built up a support network over the years, you should reach this point with a few people willing to read your dissertation and offer feedback. Take their comments to heart and revise as needed. Once you have edited and revised your dissertation into its third, possibly fourth, iteration, ask your PhD advisor to review it. They will undoubtedly have comments and suggestions. Make all the corrections they give you, as they are the person you want to please the most. The fifth draft is the version you will defend.

After you proofread, print, and bound your dissertation, you must submit it to your PhD committee. Next step, you will defend your dissertation in what is known as a "viva voce." The defense is when your committee will pick your dissertation apart after combing through it indiscriminately. There could be a panel of professors and examiners external to your committee who are present to ensure your department is not simply passing anyone. Similar to your prospectus defense, this will be oral, and it should celebrate your achievement—combined with a bit of academic hazing. Be as concise as possible when you answer the question posed to you, and if you do not know the answer then answer honestly you do not know or it was outside the purview of your research. You cannot bluff these people as they have been doing this for years, sometimes decades. They will see through it and fail you if you walk into that room thinking you can. That is possibly the only way to fail a dissertation defense, as your chair should have stopped all planning if they thought there were problems with your research or writing.

The defense begins with you giving a presentation about your field, why you chose this topic, your sources, and your contribution to the world. After that, the committee will begin to pepper you with questions meant to test what you know and what you do not know. You can expect several of the following questions:

- What is your research about?
- What was your motivation for this topic? What, if any, is the personal connection?
- Why did you pick these particular sources for your literature review?
- How do your findings relate to this existing literature?
- Did your research evolve during the writing process, and if so, how?
- How did you design your study?
- Why did you take that design approach?
- What limitations did you experience as a result of your research design?
- Tell us about your study's generalizability, validity, and reliability.
- What research biases exist in your study?
- What were your key findings?
- Do you think that your research has significantly contributed to the advancement of the field? How?
- Can any of your findings be put into practice? If so, how? If not, then why?

This list is not exhaustive, and countless other questions related to your subject could come up. These are some of the most general questions you can expect, but your field and dissertation topic will dictate more specific ones. After submitting your dissertation to the committee, take the time to practice your defense with a few peers and professors who can ask questions about your study. Once again, you can never be too prepared.

After the defense is over, they will ask you to step out of the room while everyone debates your performance and dissertation. There are five responses you can typically expect: high pass with no revisions, conditional pass with minor revisions to your dissertation, conditional pass with significant revisions to your dissertation, fail with revisions to your dissertation (which means you will have to revise and redo your defense), or a complete failure. The chances of a high pass or a complete failure are low. Instead, most will pass with major or minor revisions to the dissertation that you can submit to your chair a few weeks after the defense. Once you successfully defend your dissertation and the panel is satisfied, the university will award you a doctoral degree!

Support Systems: The Gift that Keeps on Giving

During this journey, your support system will become the most important part of your life outside of your PhD committee. While the committee should be regarded as part of your support system, they are also your supervisors, not your friends. The amount of research you will complete is staggering, and you might find that days go past before speaking to a friend or family member. The loneliness will wreak havoc on your mental health, affecting your physical health as well. Humans are not meant to be in isolation for prolonged periods, but that is the life many academics force themselves into. Then, they get burned out and blame academia and not their actions. Instead, I want you to text someone if you are not up for a call, go outside and walk, go to the gym, soak in a bathtub, have sex, watch TV, keep your rest day sacred and bring people along if you can, all these things will keep this road from bringing you down. Take a complete mental break and talk about something that makes you laugh. Reminisce about old times. Talk about upcoming plans. Remove the focus from your work for that moment. Lean on your support system through every stage of the process and you will make it through.

Life can be immeasurably lonely as a PhD student, even more so for a Person of Color. While you will have many people around you rooting for you, you are on this journey alone. You research alone. You write alone. You are in complete control of your future at this point. For some, this is a liberating experience. For others, it is an immensely frightening experience. A lot of questions and emotions are going to come up. You will question why you decided to do this, why you missed your friend's baby shower or your cousin's graduation party. You are going to feel lost at times, but this should not scare you off because you took the time to prepare for all of it. Understanding that everyone goes through this and comes out better off than before should encourage you to pursue this goal. That said, keep your support system on speed dial. There is no denying that you will need them. Do not forget to take the time you need to let off some steam. It will come as a welcome mental break amidst a hefty workload. Above all, take it one day at a time, and do **not** be too hard on yourself.

Give others the gift of your time, and they will give you a respite from the life of a graduate student. Use your support system as the backbone of your journey, and you will make it to the end.

*

Earning your PhD is often seen as the final step of your academic career. After years of hard work and many moments that you thought you would never overcome, you are conferred with your degree, a hood, sometimes even a sword. Most importantly, you are now a doctor! The highest academic level of any field. However, your work is not done. Maintaining the mindset of a lifelong learner will serve you well. There is so much more that can be researched—so many gaps in current literature to fill. You will also have the opportunity to decide if you want to continue, or vie for, a position at your Alma Mater. If not, you might be moving on to an external research organization.

Your New Journey

When I was learning to shoot in the Marine Corps, they drilled into us that before we pull the trigger we need to know our target **and** what lies behind it. The same is true for life. You cannot plan to do something without also preparing for what happens after you hit your target, and I would not do a friend justice if I did not prepare them for what happens after getting their degree. So in case it was not clear, completing graduate school is just one—albeit long—step in the journey on your path toward success.

TAKING THE NEXT STEP

At this point in your life, you will begin exploring what your master's or doctorate can offer you regarding sustainable career development. Keep in mind that the trajectory of your career will always be determined and led by your goals. Now is the time to begin putting all of your plans into motion. If you followed the tips in earlier chapters, you should have a definitive, but flexible, plan to start the next phase of your career.

As you already know, flexibility is crucial at this point. Strong beliefs concerning your goals are terrific, but they should not prevent you from pivoting in your career if needed. There are so many people who stick with a decision because they spend a long time making it. People of Color are affected most by this preconditioning which tells us that we need to have certain things by a certain age. You need to finish high school at a certain age. You need to start your undergrad by a certain age. You need to be married and have children by a certain age. You need to keep up with others from another race or culture. Need, need, need; the list is never-ending. What you should understand is that there is no time limit on anything. Life is not a one-size fits all experience. If every individual is unique, every person's experience is bespoke. You have the right to change your mind. In fact, change is good. Change keeps your momentum going. I am not recommending you flake on your goals, but flexibility is always good.

If you reach this point and decide to do something else, go for it, but if you have a documented plan for success before you begin school then you already know what comes next. However, if you failed to plan accordingly—despite me telling you otherwise—you can still recover while you navigate life after graduate school. Thankfully, this next step is easier than any you have taken up to this point.

Now What?

As you complete your degree, and lift the hefty weight associated with it off your shoulders, you will experience a strange period of sadness and confusion. While you will be elated regarding your accomplishment, you might also be awash with several other, and more uncomfortable, emotions. The question ringing in your mind: "Now what?"

What happens after all the fanfare dies down and you are left with getting on with the next phase of your life? For starters, you might feel you lost a big piece of your identity as a scholar. You will no longer walk onto campus as a student again. However, this does not mean that you are no longer an academic. In fact, as a PhD holder, you are now among the ranks of lifelong scholars who are held in high esteem as you once regarded your professors when you were an undergraduate. That is why choosing a program centered on your passions and goals is so important. When you have a PhD in a field you are passionate about, there is no end to learning. There is such a wealth of information in this world and so much more that you can dedicate your research to.

Moreover, earning a PhD means you can continue working with your Alma Mater as a professor or with another university if that interests you. Countless PhD graduates become important figures in the educational system that helped them earn their certifications. Being able to evolve into any of these positions means you do not have to look back on your studies with nostalgia. You can progress into a new and even more exciting path as an academic.

Even if your interest lies outside the Ivory Tower, you should maintain the support network you fostered on campus, as they can assist you in the next phase of your career. Just because you completed your program and are planning to move into industry does not mean you have to cut ties with your support system. Hopefully, you built beautiful relationships with your chair and the rest of your committee members. I hope you do the same with several peers and fellow graduates. Maintaining close contact with these individuals is not outside the realm of reality at all. Maintaining contact with these individuals can help you transition from graduate to employee, professional researcher, or entrepreneur.

Transition: a keyword here.

Your New Journey

The transition period after you graduate is often one of the hardest you will experience, but think of it as another step in your journey. In most cases, your university will want to keep this polished gem they flourished, e.g. you. Thus, they seldom prepare you for a non-academic job. That does not mean that they set you up for failure or are maliciously trying to keep you "trapped" in their institution. It just means that most universities have objectives to meet. One of those objectives is training, and retaining, excellent academics, such as yourself. Because most, if not, all of your professors went from elementary to PhD without working outside academia; it is the only life they know. Thus, they will teach what they know and possibly push you down that route. However, it is not the only path you have to take.

While your department will want you to become a professor, you may want something else, something **more**. It is not uncommon for PhD graduates to pursue a career in industry or independent research. There is often more money and independence outside the classroom than in it. If that is what you desire, then I encourage you to speak with your professors and committee members. While they may have little to no experience with it, they will have students who graduated like you who found jobs outside of academia. Find out who among their graduates has experienced that particular transition before and whether this is something they would recommend. Whether the answer is in favor or opposed, ask them to elaborate on why they feel this way. Ask probing questions about job opportunities, pay, benefits,

Chapter 8

research independence, work/life balance, and whatever other factors are key to your life. When all is said and done, it will be your decision to make, but having this insight might help you finalize that decision. Use your network to plan early enough in your studies, and you can build your entire dissertation around achieving your career goal. However, even if you did not, you can work to recover afterward, or if your goals change you can find a way to use an industry heavy research project to teach in a classroom. It will take imagination and work, but you can get it done.

There is another keyword that we need to examine: network.

Networking is the best way forward as a PhD graduate. This statement is even more important for a Person of Color. The fifth-generation PhD holder in your cohort will have a ready-made network of employers and universities lined up to hire them before they graduate. Conversely, most People of Color do not have this same system waiting for them. Thus, the network you formed during your studies can assist you in furthering your career when you are nearing graduation.

Remember, your unique background makes you notable among academics. You are the only one like you, and more universities and employers are realizing they need diverse voices and talent to grow in the twenty-first century. Attending seminars, social events for academics, conferences, and any event where people can see you and recognize your talent are great ways for others to realize **they need you.**

Establish a network of professionals both in and outside of academia during your studies, and make sure they are all in your field so you can lean on them when needed. They will have an ear out if there are openings for diverse talent in your field, and if they know you are searching, they will reach out to you to apply. One day, you will help a fellow graduate student do the same.

Staying true to your goals and knowing your worth at this time is a must. Do not allow yourself to become the token hire. Ask questions about the new opportunity: why are they searching for diverse talent; what happened the last time they hired someone like you; how many people like you recently left; what does your future look like if you go down that route? Know yourself, what you are willing to put up with, and if this next step is best for you and your professional goals.

Once you have an idea that you are ready to take that step, you can fully explore all the careers open to someone with a graduate degree.

Career Prospects

Navigating the job market is no easy feat. Understanding what you want to do with your newly minted degree will go a long way in simplifying the process. You may think this is unnecessary since you will have set your goals before enrolling; however, not everyone feels the same about their goals once they have completed their program. You might have established your research organization only to feel as though you need a break and stable income from a job. You may realize you hate teaching, so you do not want to be a professor as you once thought. Change is expected, and I want you to be a flexible with yourself when you reach this point.

Already, you will have successfully completed a prolonged period of independent study, and if deviating from your original plan will provide you with some respite, you should do that. It will give you a couple of years to define your goals with your newfound expertise. Detours, new paths, revamping your life, these are all normal things for someone's life journey. If your definition of success evolved during your study, great! Redo your SMART goals and plan accordingly. There are numerous career prospects for someone once they finish graduate school. You have the skills to do whatever you want with your life now, so use them.

Academia

This option is safe and readily available to almost all PhD graduates. If your goals involve academia, you will find it easier to find a position with your Alma Mater or a comparable university once you have graduated. Comparable is key here, as it is quite difficult to rank up after graduating, and academia revolves around its ranking system. The first year is often a postdoctoral period and will involve at least a year of employment teaching classes similar to a TA. Postdocs can sometimes be extended up to four years and even evolve into a permanent position with the university in question.

While sticking with your Alma Mater can feel like the most logical choice, it can keep you trapped in your comfort zone. You should shake things up a little at this point. Trying to find another university in-country or abroad is the best option for you. You will meet new people in your field and get exposed to new research techniques. Your goal should be to learn as much as possible about your field. Spreading your wings, so to speak, gives you this opportunity. Additionally, postdocs make little money. While the pay is higher than the stipend you receive as a PhD student, the money is still much less than others who pursue careers or are already employed as professors. Seeking a postdoc elsewhere gives you a chance to travel on their dime while you look for a permanent posting.

Speaking of, some find employment with other universities as tenure-track professors or adjunct professors as they near graduation. They are the lucky few. There are insufficient positions for the number of graduates every year; however, many universities are looking for diverse talent to bring in more students. Thus, if you plan appropriately from the beginning of your studies, you will reach this point with all the publications, expertise, and postdoc positions needed to make yourself a viable candidate. The journey will still be difficult and require a lot of hard work, but those who make it see it as one of the most rewarding decisions of their life.

Chapter 8

Academia is not for everyone, however. If you have children at a critical stage of their scholastic lives, a spouse that cannot relocate with you, or any other circumstance that might make a move more strenuous than it is worth, do not do it. Maybe you do not want to teach because you do not like the students, the pay, or the university culture. If so, then do not pursue that route. Even if others love it, do not feel pressured to conform to their standards. Additionally, there are those who really wanted to be an academic but cannot find positions open in their field. Sorry to say that even with the best preparation, you could lose out to someone else who prepared just a bit more or knew the right people to snake the job from you.

There are still numerous additional options outside academia, and the best part: most of them pay more.

Government

If you dream of making a difference in your community and the world, a government position might be right for you. Generally speaking, you would be looking at becoming a government researcher, regulator, policy advisor, politician, or analyst. Whether it is with the local, state, or federal government, the positions come with decent to high pay, guaranteed benefits, job security, and countless avenues for career growth because of the size of the government. Additionally, because the government sets the policies for how people of diverse backgrounds are treated, most organizations in the government have a high degree of diversity, equity, and equality compared to those outside. Thus, if you are worried about how you will be treated, government positions can give you a sense of security and community that may not exist in other places.

Taking on the role of government researcher will be the closest to your PhD experience in terms of work. Researchers are needed in practically every wing of the government. From forensic science to agriculture and even biotechnology, researchers utilize their skills in every facet and every level of the government. The US Department of Defense, for example, is known for hiring social science majors to expand their knowledge of human behavior. Their remuneration is excellent compared to academic positions, and tenure is much easier to acquire, especially for my fellow veterans.

If you are more interested in public affairs and consumer safety, working in a regulatory position will suit you well. You will engage with the government as well as heads of industry to come up with the most efficient regulations. These are regulations that will work toward safeguarding the general public and ensuring that industries operate ethically. The pay is high, you will be respected by many as an expert in your field, and you get to play a part in crafting the future.

Another route is policy advisory and analysis. If you have ever felt like the policymakers and politicians in your state missed the mark in their efforts, you could steer them clear of error in the future. As a policy analyst and advisor, you

Chapter 8

will give politicians and other policymakers the expertise they need to make informed decisions. This is where filling your cup first comes back into the limelight. If you recall, we discussed the importance of holding the door open for community members to follow you. We also looked at how your move into academia could encourage children from your community to pursue academics. You will become a role model for many people in your community. As a policy advisor, you could work on policies that directly affect the people you want to inspire. This will bring you full circle and become your version of filling everyone else's cup.

An added bonus to any position with the government, you will have the opportunity to pursue independent research. Typically, academics are expected to work twenty-hour days, focusing all their research and time on furthering the university. In contrast, the government has no mandate. Instead, you will work a standard eight-hour day; any research you complete outside of that is your own. Publications, lectures, and conferences will all be yours and credited to you only. If you decide to rest for a year or more, that is fine, as there is no mandate to complete these tasks. There is currently a wave of academics recognizing that they have more intellectual freedom working with the government and a better work/life balance than with some universities with restrictive research and time policies. So consider this option, and if it is right for you.

Military

If you are reading this and have not begun your graduate studies, you will be pleasantly surprised to learn the military could fund your studies. You can apply for funding to enroll in graduate school if actively enlisted. The only requirements are that you return to serve as an officer once you have graduated. If you are already an officer in the military, there are multiple programs to fund an advanced degree that simply require an extension to your time. Veterans can use the GI Bill, while grants and scholarships cover all expenses. If you were not connected to the military when you enrolled, you could still land a job with the military as a PhD graduate through a process called direct commission.

As a PhD holder, you can enter the US military at an O-3 level, sometimes O-4 if your field is highly specialized. If you have no prior military experience, you will be required to undergo military training, but after finishing, you will be a leader. Job security is top-notch, as the contract you will sign can last for years. Benefits are some of the best in the country, and you will be respected in your field. Military officers are held in high esteem by all, and the combination of both rank and degree will cement your reputation as one of the top experts in your field.

> **SIDE NOTE:** Standard monthly pay for an O-3 ranges from $7,000 to $9,500 at the time of writing this.

Be sure to speak to a commissioning officer to get the most up-to-date details and requirements if you consider this option. It is not for everyone, and unfortunately, racism is still quite prevalent in military circles. Furthermore, military life does involve commitments of your time and the possibility of sacrificing your life for the sake of others. Consider if this is truly the best route for you and your family. If you feel the call to serve, then this route allows you to do so while using your degree.

Corporate Researcher/Writer

If none of the aforementioned careers interest you, there is always the possibility of finding a position as a corporate researcher, writer, editor, analyst, or project manager, to name a few. The jobs in the corporate world are endless. Working for a research organization, non-profit organization, or small business are also on the table and they represent three lucrative career prospects.

Most corporate positions are untapped by academics because so many professors never worked in that world. Their lack of experience means they fail to introduce this possibility to their students, and the cycle continues. However, there are literally millions of companies across the planet that actively seek out people with advanced degrees to hold high-ranking positions with their companies.

Business majors can find opportunities in data science, accounting, finance, and leadership roles. Earth sciences or people with geology degrees can find a plethora of opportunities in engineering and construction. Social sciences majors can look into social work and public health. The list is almost endless. If you have a passion, there is likely a corporation with similar interests. As mentioned in an earlier chapter, browsing recruitment sites for positions related to your degree before starting is advisable., so you can build your degree around your goals. Furthermore, you should also visit job fairs at your school or conferences in your field, as you will meet hiring managers who can tell you what these corporations are looking for. Some will even conduct an interview on the spot.

Remuneration in the corporate world can be staggering. Large technology companies will offer PhD holding researchers upwards of $400,000 annually. Smaller ones often offer less, but the pay is still much higher than that in academia or the government. However, the benefits are not always comparable, and there is always the chance you can get fired for the simplest mistake. I once watched an interview with a CEO and the head of one of his departments, and the CEO fired the department head during the interview for admitting their department had flaws. Additionally, if you feel out of place in academic circles, you may find the corporate world even worse. Racism, sexism, bigotry, xenophobia, misgendering, microaggressions, nepotism, and much more are all still prevalent, and there are many cases where companies make little to no effort to correct the inequities present in the workplace. You may find a company that does not have this fault but does pay well; thus, making it the perfect fit for you. If you do, then you will find a place that will pay you what you are worth, and you can always donate money or time to your local community if you want a way to give back.

I will way this again, research, research, **RESEARCH**. Only about 20% of graduates remain in academia, so if you are considering any of the career prospects outside of academia, that is entirely normal. Remember, the path to success is bespoke, and you do not need to conform to anything that does not align with your values or goals. Think about what career prospect is best for you, and pursue it. The best plan is to have a goal when you start your journey so that you can plan accordingly during your studies. Volunteer with organizations that can help you achieve your dream job, seek internships with companies you want to work for, and look for ways to ensure your entire graduate program is geared toward your goals. You can write a dissertation knowing it will later be perfect for a corporate or government job, and when the time comes, they may even be seeking you out versus the other way around.

Resume Crafting

Resume writing is an art, one that many are not familiar with. Unfortunately, people from underrepresented communities tend to be the majority in this group as many of our parents and friends never truly mastered this craft, and the people reading our resumes do not attempt to understand this fact when judging us. Similar to the variety of fields you can apply to after graduating, there are multiple resume writing styles, each with a distinctive version of what is correct. This section will discuss a few of the most common, but you should open up your favorite search engine and type in "resume template for (fill in with specific university or career)."

Cover Letter

A Cover Letter is standard for most resumes as it summarizes the information from your resume while connecting your qualifications to the school or job you are applying for. As most decisions are made by overworked personnel who do not have the time—and sometimes the brainpower—to connect your awesomeness to the position, you must do it for them. Let that image play in your mind while writing your Cover Letter as the first person who reads it will unlikely be the person who makes the final decision since they are gatekeepers who begin the process. Furthermore, you want to make sure you use some of the keywords from the job posting while making this connection; this will further help with the first round of cuts, as whoever is looking it over may use a computer program that searches for specific phrases if they have hundreds of applicants.

The tone of your Cover Letter should be professional, and you want to write it in standard letter format. Begin with Dear... if you know their name, date, address, and end with Sincerely, (Your Name). Keep the letter to one page and all of your verbiage succinct. Thanks to Artificial Intelligence, this phase has gotten a lot easier. You can use various prompts to craft a winning Cover Letter that helps you format most of this information, but make sure that you proofread and revise whatever is created through AI as the technology has not been perfected yet. Ensure the tone remains highly professional throughout, and you should avoid using conjunctions and other writing faux pas that can seem too informal as it can give an air that you do not care as much as others.

The first paragraph should introduce you and have three additional sentences which connect to the topic sentence of your following three paragraphs. Those three will be the body of your Cover Letter, and each has a purpose. The first body paragraph discusses the needs of the company or university that you are applying to. Avoid mentioning yourself, as this is meant to show you understand what they are looking for. The second paragraph discusses your qualifications and their relevance to the position. Connect this paragraph with the previous one to show why you fit their needs perfectly. The third should show you know something about the company or university (something you can search while writing), and you want to clarify that you are purposely applying because of this anecdote and others. End it with a concluding paragraph summarizing at least two key points while thanking the letter reader for taking the time to read your Cover Letter.

Academic Resume (For Graduate School)

Applying for graduate school can be daunting, and most are doing it while still in undergrad. This means you may have yet to work or apply for a job that requires a resume. Furthermore, they will want experience or qualifications you may have yet to earn since you are a young student. (Why do some of them ask for published papers?) However, writing a resume for graduate school is easier than it initially seems. You should be creative and accentuate what you have done to make one thing clear: you have the **ability** and **drive** to finish graduate school. That is all they want to know. Prove that, and you are in.

Format for an Academic Resume is unique because you want to convey your abilities as a student rather than your skills as an employee. However, you still want to keep this to one page to ensure the screener can skim your resume and decide early on if you are qualified. Thus, your focus needs to be on education, written papers, classes taken, and job experience related to your program. We will examine take these in order.

Education needs to be the most significant portion of your Academic Resume. All undergraduate universities or colleges attended should be listed, along with your GPA, entrance and exit dates, and whether you obtained a degree. High School education is typically ignored; however, if you attended a prestigious high school that had a preparatory program or participated in a program in your high school that set you on your path toward graduate school then it is worth mentioning here as you will likely discuss it in your Cover Letter as well. For example, you were the head of the engineering team and built a robot, and now you are applying for a Master's Degree in Engineering; it can help to show this has been your passion since a young age.

In each section of your schools attended, you can have relevant classes taken or substantive papers written that pertain to the graduate program you are currently applying to. For example, if you took Biology 302 (Marine Biology) and Biology 402 (Advanced Marine Biology), and wrote two papers in your 402 class then you want to list this under the university in which they were completed and the significance of that paper.

Find a format that works best for you, and research the university you are applying to, as they may have a format required for student resumes. Follow their template to the letter, as they may use a computer filter that will automatically reject your resume if it does not follow their prompts. However, most will have open resume formats. The next page is an example of what you should write.

University of **Awesomeness**	August 2023- May 2027
Bachelor of Arts, **Philosophy**	G.P.A. **4.4** out of **4.5**

Relevant Coursework:
Phil 101 (Intro to Philosophy), Phil 103 (Socratic Method), Phil 212 (Rene Descartes' World), Phil 312 (Advanced Philosophy)

Relevant Papers:
"I Think, Therefore I Can Pass: A Case Study of Descartes and Modern Academia." Phil 312 Capstone, available as a writing sample, 32 Pages

"Appealing to the Masses: How to Make Philosophy Digestible Again." Undergraduate Thesis, available as a writing sample, 56 pages.

Table 3: Resume Example

Notice the white around specific sentences. How I use bold lettering for the heading but leave the other sections in regular font. These contrasts make the resume easier to read and give it a bit of beauty when printed out. Furthermore, it can help someone skim through to find the most essential information so they know you belong there. For example, if they are looking for GPA and degree, they will see both within seconds and put your resume in the "keep" pile before moving on.

Chapter 8

Secondary to education is work experience, unless you have a lot of it. Most students will have little to no relevant work experience, but since you listened to me, you will have prepared before applying and worked an internship or volunteered with an applicable organization. If so, you want to write out the job, dates worked, and tasks similar to what you expect in graduate school. For example, you assisted a paralegal in researching a case in the state law library, and now you are applying for law school. Put that here, and if you know the number of hours worked, put that here as well. Make it clear that you did the job well and plan to do it even better in the future.

There are a few, like me, who worked multiple jobs before applying to graduate school, which have no relevance to your current application. Your time at the local movie theater looks excellent if you are applying for film school but seems out of place if you are applying to medical school. However, if you worked some strenuous positions, worked somewhere you are proud of and hope to discuss in your academic interview, or served in the military, then you want to list those jobs because they help show you can finish graduate school. If listing the job will not help you, then do not add it to your resume as it will detract from your submission.

Connect your Cover Letter to your Academic Resume, and show—do not simply tell—that you have the skills and the drive to finish the degree you are applying for. Nearly everyone applying is smart enough and has the grades, but a lot of people start extempore and leave graduate school when things get tough. We already know you are not one of them because you prepared by reading this book first. Now you have to show them that.

Curriculum Vitae

So, you want to be a professor. That is Great! However, it is a long road, one fraught with long nights and sometimes longer days, and it all begins with applying for the job.

The Curriculum Vitae (CV) summarizes your education, classes taught, academic achievements, job experience, and contributions to the field. It is the longest form of resume in existence, and there are endless ways to format one. The longest CV I have seen was 91 pages, listing everything that person had done in their thirty-year career, from book reviews to classes taught. While that may seem ridiculous to some, that is the point of a CV. You want to convey that you are that one-in-a-million person, and the university you are applying to needs you more than you need them. However, let their needs be your guide and think of ways to limit your CV. If you can write ten pages relevant to the position, then focus on those ten and bring up more during your interview. You can also have more information on your website should they want to review it.

If you are a recent graduate then focus more on your education, but if you have some time in the field or published a few papers, focus on those instead. Additional headers should include relevant coursework, articles published, classes taught, classes taken, papers presented, television interviews, books published, manuscripts in preparation, languages spoken and written, previous work experience, invited lectures, fields of research, labs worked, legal battles won, surgeries performed, and many more. Academics come from all walks of life and do an unlimited number of things because of the various fields in existence. Thus, there is no one way to write a CV; however, no matter your field, you want to convey that you are one of the best. If your CV does not make that clear, then they will not call you for an interview.

Universities will ask for up to a dozen additional documents when applying; some are easier to gather than others. These documents include: a Diversity, Equity, and Inclusion Statement; all university transcripts, three to six letters of referral; two or more writing samples (typically a published paper or book chapter); proposed course syllabi; Teaching Philosophy; Cover Letter; and in the case of private institutions, a statement on your religious or political beliefs. The university or college you are applying to will have all the required documentation in their job posting, and most will only look at your application once their system marks your package as complete. Thus, you will have to gather all of these additional documents for every position you apply for.

Research the university you are applying to and look for examples of successful applicants who posted their resumes online. Reach out to them if possible, and ask them what worked and what did not. Even better if they have a similar background as you because they may be willing to help you get your foot in the door.

Government Resume

You suit. After spending your teen years railing against the "man," here you are, considering applying to become one of them. Luckily, nearly everyone regrets their adolescent decisions, so nobody will hold it against you.

The US has three hiring levels for the government: federal, state, and local. The federal government has one of the easiest application processes that I have seen, and they do not require you to enter information already on your resume. Government resumes tend to be about seven pages, but they can sometimes be longer. Sections can include everything on your CV, and have additional information, such as if you currently have a security clearance and your citizenship. By accessing USAJobs.gov, you can build your resume on the website and apply to every job you think is appropriate with a few clicks. However, you want to ensure your application is worth their time.

Contrary to academia, your education and teaching are not the focus; instead, you want to focus on job experience and skills. I have seen tenured professors freak out when applying to the government because they think they have no skills outside of giving a lecture, but they ignore all of the transferable skills professorships have. The same can be said for nearly any job you have previously worked. You should list every job worked, dates of employment, hours worked per week, and your salary. Then under that, you need three bullet points that make it clear you learned **at least** three skills at that job that are transferrable to the job you are applying for, or at the very least, you accomplished some essential tasks while working there. Look at this example:

Contract Writer, 40 Hours PW   August 2020-Present
America's Historian, LLC $98,000 Annually
• Wrote the 2021 Annual Study for AH after learning the Chicago Manual of Style Writing Guide. The study was successfully written and published one month ahead of schedule thanks to my efforts, which led to an end-of-year bonus of $10,000.

Table 4: Skills & Work Experience Annotation

Notice that a hiring manager could look this over and quickly learn where I worked, what I did, hours worked, and time worked, and then move on to the amazing job I did there. Similar to the bullet point above, you want to convey a lot succinctly. That one bullet point demonstrates I learned a new writing style and then wrote a major annual study which I completed a month early, and my boss must have loved it because they awarded me a $10,000 bonus for it. Two more bullet points like that, and they will know why I am one of the best candidates for the position.

Even people who have only worked in academia can write a similar statement as you have learned new skills, presented them to audiences ranging from students to other experts, and received awards for your efforts. This example is only one of over a hundred ways to present work experience, but I used it purposely to show you can focus on your abilities while demonstrating work experience. Research additional examples, consult friends and others who have found jobs in the government, and ask hiring managers for feedback if they turn you down for the job.

Government positions will require additional documentation, but not nearly as much as academic positions. If you are a veteran, they will want your discharge paperwork, SF-15, and all applicants will submit unofficial transcripts. You can include names and contact information for referrals in your resume, but most jobs will not require that. If the position requires a background check, they will gather that information after you are tentatively offered the job and contact those people when appropriate.

Be warned, it can take a long time to get a job with the federal government because the hiring process is slow, and checks are even slower. You may have to get another job while waiting.

State and local governments have similar hiring processes. They will have websites and post their jobs on different job boards, but your focus should be their website and hiring forum. Similar to the Federal Resume, you want to focus on your skills and abilities, and you want to present yourself as an expert (which you are thanks to your degree).

Some states are faster than others because they have a streamlined hiring process, and each has required documentation for permanent and contract positions. Furthermore, depending on where you live, you may be subject to drug tests or other pre-screening that others will not have to do. However, you will see all of those steps on your state website, which is why I want you to focus on there instead of a job board which will summarize a lot of information. I do not want you to be surprised once you start applying. With that said, if you are looking to move, job boards can be a great starting place to find which state is hiring, and then you can focus on that state's website once you identify your next home. The same can be said for local governments, but many prefer to hire locals who already live in the area and are familiar with the people. That is not true for all, so it is still worth looking into. Just do not get too upset if they reject you if you are not a local; most do not have the budget to pay for moving expenses anyway.

Connect your skills to your Cover Letter, and demonstrate that you are a hard worker willing to learn more and replicate your past success. No matter what your past work experience is, you should be able to make that point clear. Thus, everyone from professors to newly minted master's with no work experience can present themselves as viable candidates for the government.

Corporate Resume (1-Page)

The government was not bad enough, you want to be a corporate snob? Damn I love you. Just make sure you remember me when you are the next CEO, as my kids will need a job one day.

A Corporate Resume is the most standard form of resume; one you will have encountered years before you decided to become an academic. Now that you have your master's or doctorate, simply add those line items under your education section while adding additional skills in your work experience section. The format is one page, two if highly experienced, and you can use the same bullet trick I pointed out in the previous section to convey your ability to work hard for the corporation you are applying for.

The sections in your resume include education, experience, and skills. Keep your resume focused on these three sections as you do not have a lot of space, and nobody likes it when someone changes the font to eight, single-spaced, and crowds the document to unreadability. By staying laconic, you can present all of the pertinent information, and whatever you do not have space for, make a note of it so you can bring it up during the interview process.

There are a few things to keep in mind when applying to corporate positions. First, you want to show them your time in academia prepared to work this job. This demonstration is straightforward for people who earned related degrees, such

Chapter 8

as an MBA applying for management. Still, even someone with a PhD in Philosophy can demonstrate why an insurance company needs a philosopher examining business ethics on their staff. Thus, focus on how you present your degree and show how your skills transfer. Second, be prepared for some hiring managers to think you are overqualified for the position. Some of them worry that a candidate who is too qualified will leave once they find a better job (which is your right), and they will use that as an excuse to not hire you. If done, ask what job someone with a graduate degree would better be suited for in the company, and push them to hire you for that position if open. Even if they do not hire you, then start applying for that role at other companies, as you may be looking too low on the totem pole. Third, prepare yourself for the corporate hiring process. There could be three or more rounds of interviews, explaining yourself and your skills to each. Furthermore, they may ask for additional paperwork as you progress along the hiring path.

Your Cover Letter is essential to the Corporate Resume because it is the only place you can connect your work experience with the job you are applying for due to space constraints. Ensure both documents speak to one another, and have a few friends look them over. Ask them what seems unanswered after reading both together, as the questions they have will show if you demonstrated why someone should hire you.

Non-Profit or NGO Resume

You are going to save the world, or at least some small part of it which you currently occupy? You? **I truly hope you are successful.**

Non-Profits or Non-Government Organizations are always looking for researchers or people with graduate degrees to lead initiatives and programs as they are the expert who has the skills to present critical information to a wide-ranging audience. You can also volunteer with one while you have a separate career. That said, the choice of organization is limitless in terms of scale and location, making it very difficult to give general advice. However, I will provide you with some pointers anyway, as I really do hope you can make the world a better place.

This resume is both like and unlike every other resume we discussed prior. You want to show your teaching and presenting abilities (similar to a CV), but you do not want to be only a teacher. Similarly, you want to show you are a hard worker with numerous skills (similar to a Government or Corporate Resume), but you are not applying to work in an office or help someone turn a profit. You are looking for the balance between these extremes.

You can use any format when writing your resume here, but most will have a particular format they are looking for. Some will ask for one page; others will say as many as you like. No matter the layout, you will want bullet points or thesis statements under your education and work experience that show all relevant abilities.

Depending on the type of Non-Profit or NGO, you will want to have differing sections. If they focus more on research, tailor your resume to present your research skills, education, writing, publications, lab work, etc., and present yourself as an excellent researcher. If they need a new project leader, impress upon them your skills in creating your degree plan, completing your degree project, the multi-year steps involved, and show that you already know what it means to lead a large project. If you were lucky enough to lead some large projects in graduate school, then detail what it was and what you did as the leader. Research the position and organization to make sure you know what they are looking for so you can craft your resume appropriately.

Your Cover Letter should show your passion. When discussing their needs think of how they need you to help them research or lead this particular project and why nobody else on the planet can help them complete this the way you could. Demonstrate why you are foregoing using your degrees to pursue another field. Let them know that your passion for research or the project is what is driving you more than anything else, and if you do so correctly, they will want to hire you on principle.

The Imposter Returns

The little voice in your head starts up again: "What if they made a mistake? What if I am not meant to have my degree? What if I just made it, and I do not know what I was talking about in the defense? I felt like I was winging it. I still feel like I am winging it. What if someone sees through me?" Seriously, **fuck that voice**.

Unfortunately, the little voice that spurs your feeling of being an imposter lives on after you earn a graduate degree. Some might say it becomes worse at that point because it is also coupled with all the emotions you experience during this transitory period from student to worker. Made worse because you might have felt out of place during the journey, and now, you are worried they finally figured out they made a mistake all along. However, no one is going to walk into your home and pull your certifications off the wall. No one is going to come and tell you that awarding you those degrees was a big ruse. You have earned them; repeat it to yourself: "I earned my degrees. **I worked hard**." When those words do not work, there are a few other approaches you can take.

Let us start with a critical assessment. One thing that your inner critic loves to do is exaggerate. It will pick apart every single one of your weaknesses and tell you that these are why you cannot possibly be successful—it is all just one big joke and the doctorate police are on the way to take you to academic jail. You should take stock of yourself to stop this

Chapter 8

inner critic from taking you down a spiral of full-blown imposter syndrome. Use a personal SWOT analysis to determine whether there is any truth in the statements wafting through your psyche. **SWOT** stands for strengths, weaknesses, opportunities, and threats. For this exercise, you will focus on your strengths and weaknesses, leaving opportunities and threats for the next phase of your journey. So, not so much a SWOT analysis as it is an SW analysis—a SWanlysis if you will.

Take some time to sit down and write your strengths and weaknesses in terms of your academics or career. Really focus on those strengths, but also give your weaknesses some attention. Do not just list them out. Make a list of ways that you can work on those weaknesses, and then take proactive measures to do just that.

How does this help?

Well, you are a logical and analytical thinker. You have honed those skills throughout your time in graduate school. When you have this data that overwhelmingly and undeniably proves that your inner critic is wrong, you will silence the imposter. You will also discover your weaknesses, and you can take steps to work on yourself, reassuring you that you are doing your best. You can also do this analysis and correction while you are in graduate school or after, and you need to convince yourself that you are truly worthy.

Remember, imposter syndrome thrives off your need for perfectionism. Accepting that you are worthy and deserving of this position that you are in will get you past the hurdle of perfectionism. Equally important is the belief that nobody is perfect. Do whatever you need to do to assure yourself of this. Imagine the dean passing gas while messing up a speech. It sounds puerile, but it will allow your mind to see people for the imperfect beings that they are. When you remove them from the pedestal you placed them on, you will permit yourself to be equally imperfect. Moreover, the dean passes gas and messes up speeches all the time, just like everyone else, so it is not like you are imagining a work of fiction or anything malicious.

Another avenue is accepting your thoughts at face value and taking over the world. If you somehow tricked every professor and your university into conferring you a graduate degree, then you can do anything! You can trick any job into hiring you. Trick your boss into giving you their job. Trick the president into making you their vice. Who can stop you? After all, you are the ultimate trickster.

If the feeling persists, you can take a different tact to rid yourself of or placate imposter syndrome. If you hear your inner critic telling you that you are a no-good procrastinator, listen to it. Have you experienced procrastination in the past? Is it something that you still struggle with? If so, your inner critic is making a valid point. Sometimes the worst emotional pain we can inflict on ourselves is trying to fight the imposter

Chapter 8

within. It can feel like swimming upstream against strong currents that keep pulling you under. When you can look at something head-on and own it, it loses its power over you. So, say, "Yes, I procrastinate from time to time. So what?" If anything, your procrastination is tied to your need for perfection. You feel wholly underqualified to tackle the task in front of you, which gives you anxiety, so you put it off for a few days and then kick yourself for doing that after. However, you still get it done every time. Whatever so-called negative aspect of yourself that your inner critic chooses to focus on could be an area that you can master. You can focus on those weaknesses, as you will have discovered in your SWOT analysis, and focus on converting them into strengths. If you find that you cannot accept them as part of your flaws, flaws that everyone has, then do something about it! In the words of Maya Angelou, "If you don't like something, change it. If you can't change it, change your attitude." You can either accept some of your flaws or that your imposter syndrome is pointing you toward something that you need to work on.

All of these are different ways to handle this feeling, and you can look for others that work for you if none of the suggestions in this book help. No matter what, this is not the time to compare yourself to others. That is the food that feeds the soul of imposter syndrome. Comparison leads to competition, while healthy if kept in check, competition can lead to envy. That can lead to many other negative emotions and behaviors that will hamper your progress. Instead of being competitive and comparing your transition to others, reach out to others whose progress you admire. Ask them how they are coping with the transition and if they have also been dealing with imposter syndrome. Be authentic in your engagement with others, and you will quickly reap the rewards. They will be able to share their experiences and provide you with pointers to help you overcome your battle with imposter syndrome. If they have stepped into the next stage of their career, they might have some tips regarding the job-hunting process or a lead at the organization that they are working with.

Once you feel like the transitory period and subsequent imposter syndrome are handled, you will find that searching for potential career prospects is much simpler. Trying to approach institutions and organizations when your emotions are running high, and you feel unconfident about your abilities will produce negative results. You must deal with that inner critic as quickly as possible and realize that this may be a recurring theme throughout your life. You will thrive in your career when you have acknowledged it, accepted it, and found a way to work through it.

*

By planning your career prior to attending graduate school, you can build your resume while attending classes. Volunteer, work as an intern or graduate assistant, apply for entry-level positions or post-docs, or find an apprenticeship of some kind. You have the power to earn years of education and experience at the same time, and when the time comes, nothing can hold you back.

You might experience a time of sadness and a sense of loss when you complete your studies. There is often this sense of never being able to go back and relive the incredible highs and lows that were a part of this period in your life. This can be prolonged if it is difficult to find employment after graduation. However, the downsides of life do not last very long, and a rainbow is always on the horizon after the rain. There are numerous jobs out there, and you will find one that is best for you. **DO NOT SETTLE!** You did not do all of this work to be a barista afterward (although I love a good cup of coffee). Plan from the beginning of your journey what career you prefer, and work toward your goal at every stage so you are one of the best candidates on the market when you reach the end of your studies. The career prospects examined in this chapter are not your only options. The next chapter gives advice for starting a business or working as a freelancer. Being self-employed is possibly the most independent job for an academic and gives you a sense of freedom you cannot find anywhere else.

BEING YOUR OWN BOSS

You have worked for someone else for years. People of Color have disproportionately been part of the working class because of systematic racism, which relegated many to generations of service jobs. Most of us entered the workforce as teenagers. You may have even purchased a copy of this book because, like me, nobody in your family earned a doctorate, so you have no one to lean on and ask for advice about the journey. After generations of working for others, you are keen on further breaking away from your family, and instead of working a job or career, you want to be the one in complete control of the business.

I got some news for you my friend, there are a lot of opportunities for someone with an advanced degree to earn money where you are your own boss.

Starting a business can be one of the most rewarding—but also the most stressful—projects you ever undertake. The good news is that you already know how to navigate the early stages of being in uncharted waters. Even if it does not seem like it, graduate degrees teach you more than just your field; the journey also teaches and enhances critical thinking, independence, networking, money management, mentoring, oral and written communication, discipline, speaking ability, and dedication. These are all skills vital to entrepreneurs; for some, they take decades to cultivate them before they see results. Conversely, you will already have them before you graduate, no matter your field of study. Additionally, creating your own business circumvents gatekeepers who attempt to maintain the status quo. Through challenging yourself and being your own boss, you are the one in control.

Another major benefit of starting your own business, launching a research organization, or even freelancing is that you will have complete management of your career and time. You will steer everything from how quickly you develop to how much money you can make. Finding potential clients, partners, and collaborators will be straightforward because you will already have several worthwhile connections, which you will establish during graduate school if you follow this guide.

If there is anyone out there who has the mental fortitude and leadership skills to start a business, it is you. Going through graduate school requires you to think calmly and rationally during mentally and emotionally straining times. Having that self-awareness and emotional intelligence will make you an indelible adversary in any field. You know how to learn and optimize systems using research. You can take harsh criticism and whittle it back until you have the lesson you need to learn in the underlying feedback. You can identify trends, experiment, and manage multiple ongoing projects. You are not "just" an academic; you are a powerhouse and a force to be reckoned with. Now, give **yourself** your due respect and start pursuing the entrepreneurial career you have always envisioned.

Full disclosure before you read the following chapter: I am **not** your financial advisor, and I have **no** fiduciary responsibility for your actions. Research what is best for your life, state, and country as the following chapter is general advice and a starting point. There are hundreds of steps toward starting your own business, and you **need** to learn all of them before you begin this path.

Building an Empire

Start with your idea. Is there a specific line of research, innovative product, or service that you thought of during your graduate studies? Many graduates often find creative solutions to real-world problems while working on their thesis or dissertation. As such, you could find yourself in a position where your research shows that not only would this solve a problem, but also become profitable for you. Your next step involves drafting an official business feasibility document, often called a business plan. This document should include information pertaining to:

- ◆ An executive summary of your business.
- ◆ A description or organogram of your business.
- ◆ What daily operations will entail, including operational hours.

- Details of your market strategies, including market positioning, promotions, and price.
- An in-depth competitor analysis.
- A development plan for your product or service.
- A management plan, including staffing solutions.
- A financial plan, including required startup and operating capital for the first year of operations.
- A balance sheet of all directors involved in operations.
- A five-year financial plan.

If you think entrepreneurship is the right choice for you, check in with your committee members. Remember, you do not have to cut off contact with them when you graduate. They can provide you with information regarding potential office space that is available to graduates. Certain universities have initiatives allowing graduates to use on-campus facilities to bring their product or service to life. Tapping into these resources will make for a smooth transition from academia into entrepreneurship. You may still have access to the support you once had, such as libraries and laboratories, to further your research and viability studies. However, universities will require some acknowledgment of their facilities and possibly a percentage of the proceeds. If so, they will fund your prototype phase, market your product or service to potential investors, and act as your first financial benefactor. If your university does not offer these resources, there might be a bank or funder your university is affiliated with that can be accessed through alum networks. Remember that your university wants you to succeed after you graduate because it makes them look good, so any reputable graduate degree-granting institution will have some program to help, you just have to ask.

An alternative is to find another source of money to fund your research. There are multiple areas you can look from the government, banks, credit unions, investors, other researchers, friends and family, or even working a job to use that money to fund your business. All are applicable, and entrepreneurs have successfully utilized each in various fields. Ask yourself, which is best for you and your business, and once you think you know RESEARCH! I know, it is the most overused word throughout this book, but I stress it to you because too few people research what is best then they fail. Since we plan for you to thrive, I want to make sure you do not follow a similar path. Instead, you will research the process to get a loan from a bank or even your parents, the paperwork involved, how it changes your business filings, when you must begin paying them back, and every minute detail involved before you ask anyone for a penny. Build your SMART goals once again, and you should have a plan for every step of the process. If it looks like one avenue is no longer feasible after you research it, find another. There is no one way to fund a business, and you want to make sure however you do it will enhance your life, not hamper it.

Whether you will be starting on your own, with the help of your university, or with a third-party benefactor, you will need to find a market for the product or service that you are planning to launch. Identify your target audience or customer base, learn who your competitors are, examine the current market share, and debate how you can best enter the business sphere. Your research skills will come in handy in this phase. If you already know that your product or service is viable in theory, conducting further research in terms of market trends will be your next step. Knowing when and how to launch your business and its offerings are essential. Using your new degree or certificate in a field relevant to the company, and showing proof of your research, will motivate financial institutions to back you, but they will want to know your business will be profitable. Marketability will be critical toward this path, and you may need outside help to ensure you can market your product appropriately.

Once you have tentative funding and have begun working on a prototype of your product—or beta version of your service—you need to consider your rights. As an entrepreneur, having the correct copyrights and trademarks, where applicable, is non-negotiable. Anything worth innovating is worth protecting. You will be protecting your financial future and your legacy by doing this. If you have not registered a business at that point, get onto that with a sense of urgency. It is easier for someone to steal intellectual property from an individual than from a well-documented business. Technically, if that happened, you would still have the same grounds for legal recourse. However, people tend to think twice before crossing a company. The same cannot be said if they regard it as an idea you have no backing for.

Registering a Limited Liability Company or a Corporation for your service or product is essential to protecting you, your research, and your financial future. Research which is best for you as both have different meanings for tax and business purposes. Furthermore, there are numerous legal responsibilities that you will have to factor into your decision making. Learn them all.

Legal Responsibilities

Being a graduate does not give you free rein to do as you please with your research. You are no longer part of an academic institution as an entrepreneur. Thus, you will be responsible for the legal aspects of your business.

If you do not have a master's or doctorate in a business-related field, this can feel like an overwhelming step. Thankfully, you have just graduated from a university that most likely has an entire department dedicated to business studies. As such, you can speak to a business professor or even an undergrad about the best route for a business like yours. Do not give your entire idea away. Just provide them with enough information on the industry and the type of services you intend to offer. You can then pick their brains on the best business structures for your business and the registration process. You may have to pay them, but it is worth it if done correctly. Some universities offer free consultations in this regard as well, so there are several avenues you can take to ensure you research the legal steps required in your state or country.

While we will not get into the finer details of business structures—because that is not what this book is about—we can still look at them briefly.

Structure	Overview
Sole Proprietorship	Easy to set up. Business owner carries all the liability. Personal effects can be seized to settle defaulting debts.
Partnership	Easy to set up. Business owners share costs, duties, and liability equally.
Limited Liability Company (LLC)	Harder to set up. Owners carry none of the business liability and will not be personally pursued for defaulted debts.
Corporations	Harder to set up. Great for companies that focus on solving social and environmental issues. Great for companies that intend on expanding to public listing status.

Table 5: Understanding Business Structures

As you can see, you can create several business structures, and all have legal and tax responsibilities. Additionally, this list is not exhaustive as you could face country-specific structures and laws outside of the United States. Your entrepreneurial goals will affect which of these structures you choose, and I suggest researching each before you make any decision.

> **SIDE NOTE:** 20% of startups in the US fail within the first two years of creation. This number jumps to 45% by year five. However, the majority of business owners who fail do not have graduate degrees.

If you are concerned about the statistics that give entrepreneurship a bad rap, consider that most business owners lack the qualifications you will have. While this does not automatically make you a better fit for entrepreneurship, it makes you more prepared. You already have the necessary skills to work under pressure, develop a research plan, and learn from trial and error. Graduate training works to your advantage because many business owners do not have these skills when they start. Furthermore, many businesses are started with no detailed plan, which plays a significant role in the catastrophic failure that some of them experience. In contrast, your graduate school journey will teach you how to research and prepare years in advance.

Now, let us talk tax. It is imperative to get your tax reporting right from the word beginning. Remember, taxes took down Al Capone, so if they can get him, they can also get you. Everything from seed funding to operational funding and so-called "soft loans" from friends and family must be documented through a business account. All business-related expenses need documentation as well. Unless you register a sole proprietorship, you and your business will be considered separate legal entities. Furthermore, no matter which

Chapter 9

structure you select, you and your business will be taxed differently on an individual and business level, respectively.

Each state has a specific way of taxing businesses in the US, and the bank you set up your business account with can help with this process. Use a processing system to track expenses and income and ensure you follow all state tax regulations.

Federally, the tax system is universal and fairly easy to understand. Once again, your bank can assist you with this process, and the IRS also details all the steps required on their website. Follow all applicable rules, as there are severe penalties for failing to follow federal tax guidelines.

Outside of the United States, you may encounter thousands of tax codes. Thus, I suggest researching that country thoroughly and how they tax businesses there. Some countries will imprison someone for failing to follow applicable tax codes, even if it was a simple mistake, so please make sure you know them all. Ask other researchers and business owners in that area if you are unfamiliar with the laws.

Lean on your networks, speak to bank representatives, look online, and research everything before you take a single step. Do not listen to an internet guru who says, "just jump in and figure it out later," as many people hurt themselves financially following a path with no plan. After following all applicable laws and regulations, you can think of ways to open and grow your business.

Taking It to the Next Level

Taking your business to the next level as a graduate degree holder is far easier than it is for someone who has not undergone the rigorous educational process that you have. You already know how to take the work of others, pick it apart, and add to it in order to make it better. Scaling your business follows the same principles. In this instance, however, you are picking apart your operations and business plan to find areas for growth.

Keeping your finger on the pulse of market trends and global issues is essential for any business. However, it is easy to get bogged down in the daily operations and lose sight of this. By starting your own business, you can give back to the institution that helped you while using talented people to boost your industry knowledge. How do you do this? You start enlisting the services of other up-and-coming graduates in your field. You can hire them as consultants, giving them flexible hours that allow them to work on their respective programs. You can hire someone who recently graduated on the recommendation of faculty members who made up your special committee. You could give someone an internship to boost their resume. You can bring a research partner in. There are many options available here. Furthermore, if you come from a marginalized community, you can ensure your business hires from that community to give more people like you a voice and a career. You can use your success to help others succeed, and honestly, it is one of the best feelings in the world when you can give back.

Marketing your business is vital to its success, but you cannot position yourself as the best option to fulfill someone's needs if you do not know and understand them. Other than research partners, business partners are also a viable option for you. You do not necessarily have to bring someone on board or have them form part of your company's directorate. You can find businesses that offer complementary products or services to partner with. Growth will allow you to tap into new markets you would not have had access to. More importantly, you can do this without altering your current products or services—or launching new ones. The next time you are in a well-known fast-food restaurant, look at the branded soft drink products they sell exclusively. That is an example of a complementary partnership, and you can follow a similar path with your business. At the least, they can help you understand the needs of diverse customers. Speaking to your previous academic support system about whether or not there are graduates in their ranks with emerging ideas could lead you to your next partner, and if not, then at least you made them all aware of your business and furthered your marketing goals.

> **TOP TIP:** In the early days of operating your business, tap into more affordable labor. Graduates might be looking for internship opportunities. Who better to assist your efforts than someone in your field? Other than them, look into freelancers early on in their careers who might be willing to work for half the rate of a new hire.

Freelancing

Not all business owners are building a corporation, some are creating a service where they work for themselves through working for others. The wonderful world of freelancing: it is not for everybody, and it is not as glamorous as one might think if unprepared. However, it is a great way to broaden your horizons, set your schedule, earn money when you want, and even travel the world for free if done right. Additionally, you can do freelancing while in graduate school or soon after graduation to earn income while seeking a more traditional career. However, freelancing can be a great long-term career if you know how to manage your time, finances, and workload effectively. You have more flexibility in terms of the projects that you take on, and you can focus specifically on one niche that falls in line with your graduate experience.

For those who do not know, freelancing is when you work for different companies without being permanently employed there. Freelancers work from home or on company grounds and charge fees according to the requested service.

Chapter 9

You can freelance for hundreds of companies a year or just one if it is lucrative enough, and you remain your own boss.

Be aware that there are several freelancing methods, each with pros and cons. That said, there is more than enough evidence that freelancers often can triple or even quadruple their income within their first year of freelancing compared to others who immediately enter the workforce. Moreover, they are free to become digital nomads—engaging with people from all across the globe virtually and having the time to travel. There could even be cases where an international company pays for your service, and they pay for you to travel to their location to present the final product. Thus, you are now traveling the world on their dime.

Whatever your area of research, there are companies that hire consultants with your expertise. Thus, freelancing could entail any number of things in your field, and you will not have to hire employees for this business model either. Freelancing is still a business, and you will have to register an LLC or corporation of some kind and pay yourself through your company. Make sure you know which is best for your business plan, and follow all applicable tax laws where you register and operate your freelancing services.

Freelancing is a rewarding business model on several levels. For many who decide to freelance, there is no turning back. The joy of working on projects that impact the world, and being a part of that process for several clients each year, is a fulfilling experience. Freelancing can be a bridge between career moves or the only way you see yourself earning an income for the foreseeable future. Finding clientele and scaling up can be tricky, but it is well worth it. If you can move past your fear of the future and accept that people have been doing this since corporations first formed, you can sustain this career and the life that comes with it.

Picking a Niche & Method

Whether freelancing or creating a business empire, you will want to find a niche for your research that ensures your business thrives. As a graduate student, you will be accustomed to researching and writing, irrespective of your field. How much you enjoyed that writing process and how effortless you found it could lead you down the path of freelance writing. Whether you are researching reports on behalf of businesses or writing marketing copy for startups, a whole world of writing is waiting to be explored. On the other hand, consulting on a freelance basis is also an option. Having your services readily available for specific projects or short-term campaigns can provide a sustainable income for you.

> **DID YOU KNOW:** There are freelancers with a focus on human resources who make upwards of $30,000 a month over the internet? Their services include consulting with people vying for executive positions, managing organizations, and overhauling resumes.

Chapter 9

Some of you may not be interested in listing your services on a freelancing platform and believe your networking skills are sufficient to spread the word. If that is the case, you should still head to one such platform to get an idea of the services in high demand. If this is your first time entering the freelancing world, having as many resources on your side is a good idea. More importantly, knowing what other people are charging for their services will help you set your prices. There are a few things to keep in mind regarding pricing.

If you are listing your services on a digital marketplace or the internet, you have to be competitive with your pricing. While your degree will be impressive, there are other elements you are judged on, as some fakers claim similar credentials. Online, verified reviews of your skills and expertise are the main component of your credibility. The great news is that you can quickly scale this into a business if you know what you are doing. Additionally, you want to make sure it is clear you are the real deal, not a scammer who only claims to hold a graduate degree. There are marketplaces for vetted professionals with degrees like yours where you can set your fees at amounts commensurate with your qualification and experience.

Whether freelancing or creating a business offering a product, you should create a business website. In the modern age, the first thing someone does when they hear about a company is look online, and you want to be in control of the narrative of your business. Furthermore, creating a business website allows potential customers to purchase your goods or services easily. Setting up your freelancing website, page, or portfolio online will allow you to prospect for your clients during personal time and to charge a fee that you feel is worthy of your expertise. You will need to research your target audience and market your services efficiently. Every field has Search Engine Optimization (SEO) phrases that others use when searching for your product or service, and you want to make sure your website uses those so potential customers can easily find you. Register the website to your business, and use it to promote yourself and your product. Use SEO to make your business findable in your niche. Also, you want to promote yourself as an authority in your field, or nobody will pay for your goods or services.

Becoming an Authority

There are numerous opportunities that a graduate degree or certificate can help you create after graduation, chief among them is being an authority in your field. You can solidify that authority by becoming a subject matter expert and using your research to enlighten the general public, and if you are an entrepreneur, then you can monetize your authority. Thousands of doctors—of the medical and philosophical kind—have websites, blogs, podcasts, and social media accounts. Using these avenues, they dispense information that better the lives of the public. Thus, becoming an authority can make money for you while opening doors to new opportunities for your business as others hear from you.

Publishing a book or a series of papers based on your research is another way to earn an income that can make you an authority in your field. Knowing your target audience is important, because you want to adjust your research and writing to what is best for them. If you are writing a book for other academics, be aware of the tone that you use. If you are writing a book for the general public, keeping the language as light and relatable as possible is the best way to go about it. Writing a research paper and writing a book for a broad audience is not the same thing, so be sure to call in the assistance of that support team again. This time, instead of turning to a peer who is accustomed to academic language and jargon, turn toward a friend or family member who falls in line with your target audience. If they get the message you are trying to convey, then you know the message is clear. If they become interested enough they cannot put the book down, you know you are onto something.

Traditional publishers are inundated with poorly written manuscripts and notes from authors who do not know how to write. However, the thesis and dissertation process ensures you know how to write a manuscript well, which can clear some of the noise. There are hundreds of world-renowned and indie publishers for you to approach with your manuscript once finished. However, if you want more control over your work and a bigger slice of the royalties, self-publishing may work for you. Just be sure to take the same steps as a regular publisher by submitting your work to a professional beta reader and then an editor before publishing. If you have the time and the marketing dollars to put behind your work, you can climb the bestseller lists on self-publishing platforms in no time.

You could speak at seminars about your book and appear on radio shows and podcasts. Your Alma Mater may invite you to launch your book or give a speech on your journey to becoming a published author. Even without a traditional publisher backing you, achieving success with your book, or books, is still possible. Your marketing objectives will depend on what you hope to achieve. You can earn passive income as a self-published author or have the fame and accreditation that comes with public exposure. If you are comfortable with public exposure and speaking areas, this can spin off into another career path altogether: motivational speaking.

Motivational Speaking

Whether you want to take one or all of the alternative paths to career fulfillment examined thus far, you can incorporate public speaking into the equation. As someone who has overcome what must have felt like insurmountable odds to have the certification that you do, you have something that very few people have. You earned your graduate degree, and very few people can say that in the world, even less so if you come from a traditionally underrepresented community.

Your journey is one that few with your background have completed, which is why you purchased this book. Once you have reached the apex of the pyramid of formal education, look for ways to help others make that climb. Speaking to undergrads about your journey and what they can expect if they embark on it is just one topic. Another is tapping into how you overcame some, if not all, of the effects of imposter syndrome as a minority in graduate school. If you have any uncertainty, yes, you can get paid to speak and motivate others, and the proceeds should run through your business. Speaking of, you can use motivational speaking as a way to advertise your business while promoting yourself. If you have to pay for travel, or even your computer for virtual presentations, detail those costs in your business expenses for tax purposes.

You can start by doing this form of public speaking at universities. However, if you want to make a fully-fledged career out of motivational speaking, establishing a blog and utilizing social media to promote your thoughts will go a long way. Your blog or website can generate income because you can monetize it. You can offer consultation services or coaching services via your website. You can sign up to have paid advertisements displayed on your site. You can drum up a following and engage with brands to sponsor your efforts. You can launch a podcast or monetize a YouTube channel.

There is no limit to what you can achieve in the digital sphere. Once you have this presence, people will be beating down your door to book you for motivational slots.

You may have already been exposed to a similar person during your studies. Speak to your past advisors about who the university turns to for such services. Try to research and find out how this person promotes their services and their going rate before deciding if you want to go down this path. It might look like a life of glitz and glam, but a lot of traveling and planning goes into becoming a motivational speaker. Like most entrepreneurial paths, you can decide when and where you speak, giving you complete control of your schedule and income. Thus, you can ensure you have time for friends and family and maintain the best work/life balance for you and your life. So, if you love to travel and speak to groups of people, jump in with both feet!

Finding other motivational coaches and public speakers with similar qualifications is wise. Watch them, listen to them, and initially emulate them if they are that good while you find your own style. However, to avoid feeling unworthy by comparison, do not compare your efforts with others. That way, you can learn what it takes to become an authority in your field without losing motivation because others are more successful than you. If you can meet with them or attend some of their events, do that. My friends are not haters, so get to know your competition and maybe help each other grow.

Chapter 9

Scaling Up

As an entrepreneur, you have a unique opportunity: total control of your business. Whether freelancing, giving speeches worldwide, or selling a product, you will have control over how and when you scale your business up to improve your income and reach. You may wonder, if I can travel the world while attending every single one of my children's sports games and recitals, why would I ever want to give that up by growing my business? However, growth is a vital part of your journey. If you are holding this book, then you either plan to or are already in graduate school, demonstrating you are a person who strives for more in their life. While keeping a small business small seems nice at first, it will grow stagnate and you will get bored. Thus, you will eventually want to grow your business, hire more people, and increase your reach.

There are benefits to scaling your business up. Namely, you ensure more people hear of your goods or services. However, there are ancillary benefits as well. For example, as an entrepreneur, very few insurance companies will work with you. Judgment toward small businesses applies to everything from medical to life insurance. If you are looking to apply for credit to purchase a home or a vehicle, this might also be a difficult one to pull off. After all, you do not have any formal employment or steady income. Thus, banks will often balk at lending to entrepreneurs unless they meet a high-income threshold. Even then, there are often high interest rates that others working a more traditional job will not face. If you scale your business up enough, you can form an S-Corp, pay yourself a steady salary, and use that money to avoid several of these issues. If you are unfamiliar with an S-Corp, then research it thoroughly. It is a business entity that works great for many entrepreneurs and can help you scale your business while protecting your family and assets.

Another issue many people need to consider when they start their business is what auxiliary task your business will entail. Whether your business is big or small, you will have numerous tasks as the business owner, and your business itself may have to provide services you never initially intended. For example, if you are freelancing, you may have to take on work slightly outside of your field to help establish yourself as an expert. Furthermore, sometimes your niche is too narrow, and you will have to broaden it to find more work. Another example is your business sells a product your research produced, but now you have to service that product with technical and customer support. Scaling your businesses up is the best way to alleviate many of these issues. Hiring part- or full-time employees could help with the additional work as your business grows. Luckily, there are several digital courses on starting and running a business—some are free—so look into what you need to do to scale your business to the level best for you.

As a Person of Color, you should want to give opportunities to underrepresented people such as yourself, and growing your business large enough to help your

Chapter 9

community thrive is a beautiful endeavor. You can hire, inspire, and promote people who are often turned away from other companies.

That said, there is more to scaling a business than just recruiting, you need to expand your network. A common refrain throughout this book, and it is there for a reason. Leaning on your academic support system is great because if your business is related to your research, you will meet dozens—possibly hundreds—of potential clients and customers. Even if they do not purchase from your business, they could refer others to your goods or services. Thus, maintain contact with your committee, professors, and peers. Any one of them might have a lead that you can follow to diversify your business beyond the services you are offering or refer someone else to you. Keeping the lines of communication open with your department can lead to a contract with a faculty member at your Alma Mater or another university altogether. Use alum networks when you can, as these are another great avenue to scale your business up when the time comes.

> **TOP TIP:** Try to find contracts that allow you to work with multiple clients simultaneously. However, beware that you will often need to sign non-disclosure and non-compete agreements. Scrutinize the contract carefully to ensure you do not give someone else too much control over your business or you.

Your New Journey

When you are ready to grow your business, make sure that you research every single step. Every state in the US has rules for growing companies; if outside the US, then understand the rules and laws applicable to that country. Your income will grow as your business grows, but as we all know, more money does, in fact, equal more problems. Research the answers to those problems before they arise, and you will be fully prepared whenever they darken your door. Do not be afraid of scaling up; consider it as another step on **your journey toward success**.

*

Entrepreneurship will always be a logical step no matter what field you studied in graduate school. Thanks to your years of research, you have all the necessary skills to operate a business, and you only need to find a niche to thrive in. Whether venturing into a corporate field or setting up a research organization, this will be far easier for you than for non-graduate degree holders. Scaling your business will also come easier to you than others, and becoming an authority in your field will be bolstered by your graduate status. If you enjoy engaging with others, using your story to motivate your community will reward you emotionally and financially. Whatever path you choose, believe that you have what it takes—because you do.

IN CLOSING

Saying goodbye to a friend has always been hard for me. I linger and keep thinking of that one last thing I want to tell them when I should be walking away. Luckily, I wrote this book for you to read multiple times throughout your life, so we will see one another again. Nevertheless, before we part ways, I want to convey a few last-minute words that resonate with you during your new journey.

Seek out Financial Literacy

Managing your finances during and after graduate school is vital to your long-term success. As a graduate student, employee, or entrepreneur, you will enjoy the money as a graduate degree holder. Seeing the size of some of your future paychecks will feel great, and the knowledge it will only grow is amazing. However, that feeling quickly fades after the first couple weeks when you realize you now have to budget an uncertain amount to cover your living expenses and research. You may have gotten familiar with the process as an undergraduate, but it is even more critical now. Even if you have a career, treat your income and expenses as any entrepreneur would and track every penny going in and out. You should be the master of your finances. Many people from underprivileged communities never get the lessons that more privileged individuals get on managing their money, and poor money management tends to be their downfall. You will avoid that fate by learning money management early on in your journey and maintaining financial discipline Take a few business classes if you need to, but you must become financial literate. It takes practice to manage your money correctly, but if you start early, you will find it easy when you graduate.

Managing your finances is easier after living on a student budget for a prolonged period. Eventually, you will get to a point where you are setting and surpassing monthly targets. Do not fall victim to lifestyle inflation as your income grows during your journey. Instead, invest your money and plan for you and your family's future. There are hundreds of books and online seminars on investment planning, and if you do not want to do it yourself then rely on a fiduciary entity to invest money for you. Hire an accountant or a firm to teach you what to do and help you manage your money to ensure your journey is a long one. Finances are the one thing that is impossible to thoroughly plan for because emergencies will arise, but if you are prepared, you can lessen the detriment to your life. If an emergency never comes, then worst case, you have money set aside for the future.

Avoiding Burnout

On that path to financial freedom and freedom of your time, avoiding burnout is one of the most consuming but essential practices. Irrespective of the course you take in life, burnout

In Closing

can ruin your journey. Burnout—true burnout—is a medical emergency. Typically, when people say they are burnt out, they mean exhausted or on their way to burnout. True burnout is a medical event that can hospitalize a person for weeks. It is a form of emotional and physical exhaustion that can take years to recover fully. Short-term burnout that does not result in a medical emergency, such as a physical collapse or an emotional breakdown, can take months to recover. However, long-term covert stress that hides beneath the surface can result in catastrophic burnout. The question is, how can stress be covert? After all, you feel it when you are stressed, right? Wrong. Not everyone processes stress in the same way. Some people act out (fight), some people drop everything and run (flight), and some people become very still (freeze) and, eventually, suppress it. Burnout can be insidious, and you need to be on the lookout for it throughout your journey.

If you are the type of person who always feels calm on the surface while a million wars are waging inside you, you need to be extra careful not to fall victim to burnout. Being on the lookout for burnout can be difficult because it will present itself as symptoms that are normal considering your workload. The signs of burnout include:

- ♦ Feeling physically exhausted. Exhaustion should not be confused with feeling tired after having pulled an all-nighter. It has more to do with your emotional levels. If you start a project and feel immediately wiped out after reading over the outline, that is exhaustion. If no amount of sleep seems to remedy the issue, that is exhaustion. Of course, checking in with a medical practitioner to rule out underlying medical causes is imperative.

- Feeling helpless and trapped. When your mind starts telling you that there is no way out of the spiral you have found yourself in, it is time to seek help. There is a solution to every problem. It might not be a solution you like, but it is all the same. Feeling defeated and helpless is a sign that you are not coping with something in your life. Even worse, it could be a sign of depression.
- Feeling lost, detached, and alone. If you feel alone in a crowded room or around the people you care about most, that is a potential warning sign. Imposter syndrome can make you feel this way as well. Considering your other symptoms will help you decipher between the two. If you cannot solve it for yourself, seek help and let a professional diagnose you.
- Having a cynical outlook. If you are in a place where you truly believe everything in the world is awful, and you do not see a point in life or living, **seek help**! Yes, there are a lot of issues in the world, but it is not all bad. Most importantly, you are valuable to the world, no matter what stage of the journey you are on. A constant negative outlook can indicate burnout or depression, and someone could help you change your view before it is too late.

- Constant self-doubt. Another similarity with imposter syndrome. If you constantly doubt your ability to perform, assess where this is coming from. If it is just imposter syndrome then a change of outlook may suffice, but if it is burnout, you may need a professional to assess why you cannot see past your doubts.
- Feeling overwhelmed by simple tasks. Someone comes up to you and asks if you can give them the number of that great restaurant you mentioned, and you grow enraged from the question. How dare they interrupt your day? Do they see how much work you have? Being easily irritated and swept up in emotion is a hallmark of burnout.
- Procrastinating. It is time to take stock if you constantly procrastinate—whether the tasks are complex or seemingly simple. Are you taking on too much, or do you need a break?

Notice the similarity to depression and anxiety, as burnout can easily lead you down that path. Remember, these signs and symptoms will not always be evident to you. Assessing your life and career to see if you would be more at risk for burnout will help you combat it early on. If you have good family or friends, then they could look out for these signs for you. Many academics experience them all, and they let the workload push them that way.

Unfortunately for graduate students and academic researchers, four of the top contributors to burnout are common with our lifestyle. These include concerns about money and working from home and, thus, being unable to "switch off" from work. They also include isolation and concerns over job security. Other contributing factors include:

- Lack of sleep.
- Relationship stress.
- Physical health concerns.
- Being a caregiver to an immobile, dependent, or sickly family member.

While there are other contributors, these are the ones that impact the lives of graduates and people in the early stages of their careers. If you spot burnout coming on, there are steps that you can take to remedy them. At this stage, it is essential to note that this information does **not** substitute medical evaluation. Always seek the advice of your primary physician or a mental health professional if you suspect you are entering the stages of burnout, depression, anxiety, or any other mental disorder. They are all treatable, and you should not ignore them.

There are some common steps you can take during your journey to aid in avoiding burnout, and I hope they help you all:

- Taking a day off. There is a reason I stressed to you that your day off is sacred. If your day is Tuesday, then I want every Tuesday of your life to be a day off. I do not care who or what calls for you to work on that day. That

In Closing

is your day for whatever relaxing thing you need to get through the week, and keeping that day throughout your career will benefit your overall life.

- If you are an entrepreneur with sufficient savings, take a hiatus from your business. If you do not have any money set aside and need to slow down, consider where you can cut back on expenses. If you can briefly move in with a family member or friend to rest, try it. Your health is worth more than material wealth.
- If you are a student or formally employed, speak to your supervisor about what you are going through. Nearly all graduate programs have resources to help with mental health, and more and more businesses are following suit. If you are working for an employer or with a university that does not have your best interest at heart then it is time to reconsider why you are there, as they could be the problem.
- Get as much exercise as you can each week. Remember how this affects your "feel good" and stress hormones. Go to the gym, get a massage, go for a run, walk to work if that will help, but stay active throughout your journey.
- Find an activity that relaxes you and commit to engaging in it as often as possible. If you love knitting, then I want you to add a stitch to that scarf damn near daily. Cooking? Why not cook for others in your department or invite friends over to cook for them? Comrade and food, win-win. Whatever the case, if you

- have something that relaxes you that you can do almost every day, do it.
- ♦ Perhaps the most important thing you can do to prevent burnout is to take care of yourself. Those basic things that all humans need: getting enough sleep, having the sun on our skin, eating a balanced diet, and drinking enough water every day. Be unapologetic about your routine and maintain it throughout the week, including weekends. Taking care of your body helps to take care of your mind, and that will aid in preventing burnout.

No matter what stage of your academic journey you are on, it is necessary to take care of your mental health and keep that support system in handy. Mental struggles can destroy a person with amazing potential. They can set a person back ten steps when they least expect it. You owe it to yourself, especially after how much you have overcome, to take care of every facet of your health.

Is Freedom Free?

A graduate degree can give you the most financial and intellectual freedom you have ever had, but that does not mean it is a journey for everyone. You pick your research, you decide when it starts and when it ends, and you can decide what to do with your degree once you graduate. Having the time to work on your projects as you see fit and take orders when it suits you will allow you to travel, spend time with family, and more. Some academics, such as motivational speakers, prefer to travel exclusively. Thus, they see the world while others pay them. Freelancing could mean you only have work when you want to. However, there are dark sides to the journey. There are racist, misogynistic, xenophobic, and homophobic individuals who could try to block your path. Additionally, you might stumble and feel like you lost it all because your degree proved too hard, your business failed, or you could not find the career you wanted when it is done. While preparation can dramatically increase your chances of succeeding, there is no guarantee that everything will work out how you want it to.

If you remain flexible and creatively look for solutions throughout your journey, you can handle many of the adverse outcomes that can arise. For example, a racist professor can be removed through formal channels, and even informal ones thanks to the internet. If your degree is too difficult, ask your department if you can transfer to another to continue your studies. If your business failed, ask yourself why? If it is a reason you can fix, try again; if not, look for a job in a similar field. You can learn from a successful business owner what they are doing right and try again in the future. If you want to be a tenured professor but no university will hire you, look elsewhere for employment. While many universities in the US are cutting back on tenured positions, there are thousands more outside of the country that you are a viable candidate for. Additionally, private and prestigious high schools love to hire graduate degree holders to teach their wealthy clientele.

Your New Journey

You should also be open to teaching online as the digital age has expanded the number of online universities. Furthermore, you can give back to your community and teach at local institutions or tutor children who need it most. The key is remaining flexible and willing to innovate solutions to whatever problem arises during your journey. Do not let a slight fall become a stumbling block preventing your success.

Is freedom free if you must remain flexible to every little thing that can come up? The answer is that nothing is ever really free, everything comes at a cost. Achieving your goals comes at the cost of your time, money, and sometimes relationships. While true you will have academic and financial freedom unlike many from your community, there are still costs to your journey. Seek out others like you who succeeded as you plan to. Look to them for both inspiration and advice. Keep in mind there might be a career prospect mentioned here that works really well for them and not for you. Everything will come down to what you feel most comfortable with and your definition of success.

This is a personal journey, your new journey. As with anything, assess the level of risk you are willing to take and why. Your risk threshold will vary throughout your life, so reassess your goals and quests until you retire. The chances you are willing to take in pursuing financial and professional freedom will not remain the same. What you can withstand today might change when you have children or after any other life-changing event.

While freedom is never truly free, this path can offer you a unique type of freedom that others will never enjoy. Assess if it is right for you before you start, and if so, then I look forward to greeting you as an equal one day.

Believing in Yourself

You have reached the end of the road with this book, but your journey is only just beginning. Because you come from an underrepresented community, graduate school will feel lonely, daunting, and nerve-wracking. You may struggle with imposter syndrome and feel like a fraud. You might even have family or friends who attempt to talk you out of it because it is too hard or too expensive. It is absolutely imperative that you find a way to work through those emotions and silence negative people and thoughts. A great support system will allow you to move through these uncomfortable moments without feeling lost and alone. While these ideas that plague your mind will not disappear altogether, your support system will make navigating them smoother. If you do not have a strong support system, seek a new one.

Keep your armor on as you go through graduate school and your subsequent career. Wait until people prove you can let your guard down, as too often People of Color are misused in academic circles. Do **not** let others take advantage of you, your time, or your intellect. Grow your network when you can, and they will help you push back against some of the obstacles that are still prevalent in higher education.

Your New Journey

When you begin this journey, you will inevitably expect something to go wrong. You will think they made the wrong choice in accepting you, or you will later think you do not deserve your success. However, this is all part of your environment that made you believe someone with your background is less deserving than someone else. That is society's bullshit, not yours. I want you to stop waiting for that other shoe to drop. Even if it does, you will be fully prepared for it.

Having clear goals from the beginning of your journey will ensure you are on the path toward success early. You should reevaluate those goals yearly until you graduate and biannually afterward. When you are uncertain about what you hope to achieve or why you wish to achieve it, it is easy for your aspirations to fall by the wayside. Focus on yourself and the vision that you have for your life. Worrying about what you feel obligated to do for your community or family early in your academic career is too heavy of a weight to carry. You will already have so much on your shoulders, and you need to be able to work through graduate school with as little pressure as possible. Focusing on your goals and success first before you help others is okay. If you prepare yourself mentally, physically, emotionally, and financially for graduate study then your goals should be attainable.

However, it is not just your goals that will set you up for success, but also the university and program you pick. Choosing the right university should not be left to chance, and your program should align with your long-term goals. As you begin your graduate program, you will see why this is so important. Being in an environment that is conducive to your learning style is paramount. Working in a culture or system that feels like more of a comfortable fit for you can be the difference between enjoying your time and constantly feeling miserable. Moreover, it can be the difference between failure and success. Take the time to choose your university carefully. Critique them nearly as much as they critique your academic resume, and make sure they fit your life.

Once you have completed graduate school, you will have the freedom to choose your career. Do not be discouraged if you do not find your footing immediately. If you plan early in your journey, then you will have all the pieces in place for the next phase, whatever it is. Whether you seek formal employment, start a business, or freelance using your new skillset, plan early and make sure **you** are happy with the final decision.

Keep reminding yourself that you deserve to be here. Always remember that this is your life. Live it on your terms.

I Believe in You

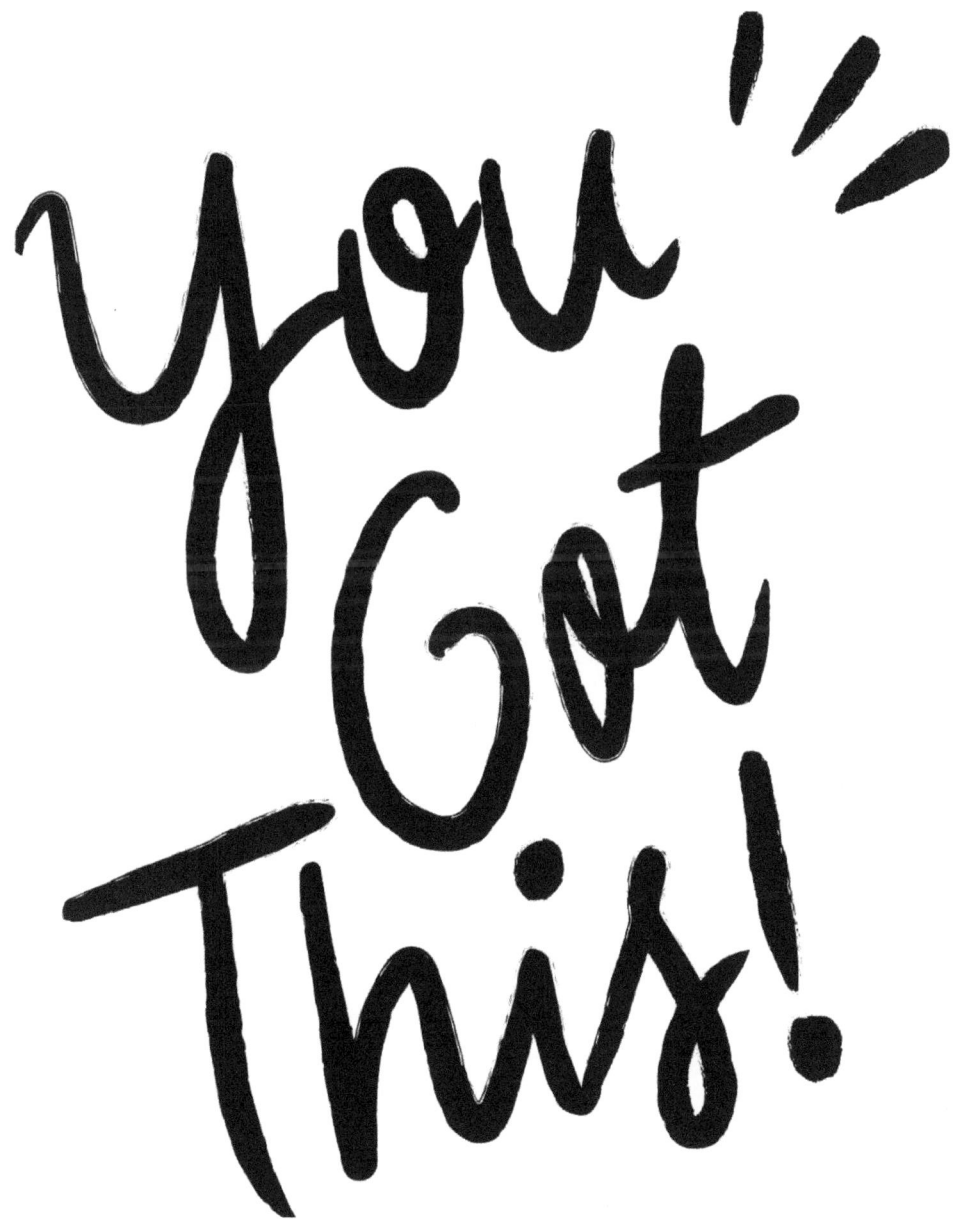

www.ingramcontent.com/pod-product-compliance
Lightning Source LLC
Chambersburg PA
CBHW040743060526
44119CB00100B/480/J